WE JEWS *and* JESUS

Exploring Theological Differences for Mutual Understanding

RABBI SAMUEL SANDMEL

PREFACE BY RABBI DAVID SANDMEL

For People of All Faiths, All Backgrounds

JEWISH LIGHTS Publishing

Woodstock, Vermont

Walking Together, Finding the Way®

SKYLIGHT PATHS®
PUBLISHING

Woodstock, Vermont

We Jews and Jesus:
Exploring Theological Differences for Mutual Understanding

2006 First SkyLight Paths Quality Paperback Edition

© 2006, 1973, 1965 by Samuel Sandmel

Preface to the new edition © 2006 by David Sandmel

For information regarding permission to reprint material from this book, please mail or fax your request in writing to SkyLight Paths Publishing, Permissions Department, at the address / fax number listed below or e-mail your request to permissions@skylightpaths.com.

Library of Congress Cataloging-in-Publication Data

Sandmel, Samuel.
  We Jews and Jesus : exploring theological differences for mutual understanding / Samuel Sandmel ; preface by David Sandmel. – 1st SkyLight Paths quality pbk. ed.
    p. cm.
  Originally published: New York : Oxford University Press, 1965.
  Includes bibliographical references and index.
  ISBN-13: 978-1-59473-208-9
  ISBN-10: 1-59473-208-6
  1. Jesus Christ–Jewish interpretations. I. Title.

BM620.S24 2006
232.9'06–dc22

2006019326

10   9   8   7   6   5   4   3   2   1

Manufactured in the United States of America

SkyLight Paths Publishing is creating a place where people of different spiritual traditions come together for challenge and inspiration, a place where we can help each other understand the mystery that lies at the heart of our existence.

SkyLight Paths sees both believers and seekers as a community that increasingly transcends traditional boundaries of religion and denomination—people wanting to learn from each other, *walking together, finding the way.*

SkyLight Paths, *"Walking Together, Finding the Way"* and colophon are trademarks of LongHill Partners, Inc., registered in the U.S. Patent and Trademark Office.

Walking Together, Finding the Way®
Published by SkyLight Paths Publishing
A Division of LongHill Partners, Inc.
Sunset Farm Offices, Route 4
P.O. Box 237
Woodstock, VT 05091
Tel: (802) 457-4000
Fax: (802) 457-4004
www.skylightpaths.com

For People of All Faiths, All Backgrounds
Jewish Lights Publishing
A Division of LongHill Partners, Inc.
Sunset Farm Offices, Route 4
P.O. Box 237
Woodstock, VT 05091
Tel: (802) 457-4000
Fax: (802) 457-4004
www.jewishlights.com

To Helen and Si

In warmest personal affection, and in appreciation of their generous support, through the Scheuer Fellowships, of scholars and of scholarship, the keystone of Jewish and Christian understanding

Contents

Preface to the New Edition

We Jews and Jesus is *not* a book about the historical Jesus. Indeed, Samuel Sandmel, my father, believed that it is impossible to recover the Jesus of history because the Gospel accounts obscure, rather than reveal, the historical Jesus with layers of later legend and theology (see chapter XVI of *A Jewish Understanding of the New Testament* [Skylight Paths Publishing, 2005]). The book is, rather, about what Jews have *thought and written* about Jesus throughout history and how contemporary Jews, informed by modern critical scriptural scholarship, might think of Jesus today. Significant portions of the world's Jews have lived, or are living, as a minority in predominantly Christian societies. They have, therefore, always been interested in the figure of Jesus. For much of Jewish history this has meant finding ways to respond to Christians who wondered why Jews did not accept Jesus the Jew as the Messiah prophesied about in the Jewish scriptures. The nature of the responses Jews have given to this question varies greatly and is influenced by both the intellectual climate of the time and the position of the Jews within the larger society.

Current events, such as Pope John Paul II's visit to Jerusalem and the publication of "Dabru Emet: A Jewish Statement on Christians and Christianity,"[1] both in 2000, the release of Mel Gibson's controversial movie *The Passion of the Christ* in 2004, and the publication of the Gospel of Judas in 2006 continue to arouse Jewish interest in Christianity and in Jesus. The increased prominence of religion in world politics in general, and of Christianity in American politics in particular, is another factor. At any given point in history, Jewish

---

[1] "Dabru Emet" was written by Tikva Frymer-Kensky, David Novak, Peter Ochs, and Michael Signer and was endorsed by over two hundréd rabbis and Jewish academics from around the world. It begins with the premise that in parts of the Christian world there have been significant changes in the theology and attitudes toward Jews and Judaism since the Holocaust. In light of these changes, Jews can now reconsider how they think about Christians and Christianity. The text of "Dabru Emet" is included in a volume of essays published to accompany the statement, *Christianity in Jewish Terms*, edited by Tikva Frymer-Kensky, David Novak, Peter Ochs, David Sandmel, and Michael Signer (Boulder, CO: Westview Press, 2000).

views of Jesus provide a valuable perspective on how Jews think about themselves, their religion, and their relationship with the broader world.[2] In this book, then, Samuel Sandmel traces the history of how Jews have described Jesus and what can be learned from contemporary scholarship, and concludes with some suggestions for Jews about how they might view Christianity in light of what has been learned over the centuries.

Samuel Sandmel, who was born in Dayton, Ohio, in 1911, was the child of Eastern European Jewish immigrants; his father escaped Tsarist Russia and the pogroms at the turn of the twentieth century. My father grew up in St. Louis and attended public schools. He graduated Phi Beta Kappa from the University of Missouri where he studied philology. He entered Hebrew Union College in Cincinnati in 1932 and was ordained a rabbi in 1937. After a brief stint as a congregational rabbi, he became the director of the B'nai B'rith Hillel Foundations at the University of North Carolina and Duke University. There he met and married my mother, Frances Langsdorf Fox. He also met and came under the influence of Harvie Branscomb III, then dean of the Duke Divinity School. When Branscomb learned of my father's desire to pursue an advanced degree in "Old Testament,"[3] he urged him to focus instead on New Testament. Branscomb understood that my father, well versed in the languages of the period and steeped in rabbinic literature and Jewish scholarship, brought an expertise to the study of the New Testament that few Christian scholars at the time possessed.

In 1942, my father left Hillel to become a Navy chaplain in World War II. Following the war, he directed the Hillel

---

[2] Two excellent articles that discuss Jewish approaches to the study of Jesus are Susannah Heschel, "Jesus as a Theological Transvestite," in *Judaism Since Gender*, ed. Miriam Peskowitz and Laura Levitt (New York: Routledge, 1997) and Jonathan Brumberg-Kraus, "A Jewish Ideological Perspective on the Study of Christian Scripture," *Jewish Social Studies* N.S. 4:1 (1997): 121–152.

[3] "Old Testament" was the term of choice in academic circles at that time. More recently, it has been recognized that "Old Testament" is a Christian term with significant theological overtones, some of which denigrate Judaism. Jews refer to their sacred scripture as Tanakh (a Hebrew acronym for Torah, Nevi'im (Prophets) and Ketuvim (Writings). More recently, scholars have attempted to find a term, such as Hebrew Bible, which, though not entirely satisfactory, is theologically neutral.

Foundation at Yale University where he also completed his doctorate under Erwin Goodenough, whose seminal work in Judaism in the Greco-Roman world greatly influenced not only my father, but all subsequent scholarship on Judaism and Christianity in late antiquity. In 1949, Harvie Branscomb, who had become the chancellor of Vanderbilt University, appointed my father to the Hillel chair of Jewish religion and thought, a position that Branscomb himself helped create and that was, at that time, one of the few chairs in Jewish studies at any American university. In 1952, Nelson Glueck brought my father to Hebrew Union College–Jewish Institute of Religion[4] where he served as professor of Bible and Hellenistic literature as well as provost and dean of the Graduate School. He retired from HUC–JIR in 1978 to become the Helen A. Regenstein Professor of Religion at the University of Chicago. Shortly after moving to Chicago, my father became ill. He died on November 4, 1979.

During his career, my father wrote numerous books and articles for both scholarly and popular audiences.[5] His scholarship and equally, if not more importantly, his ability to speak honestly but without rancor helped him become an internationally recognized pioneer in interreligious dialogue. Krister Stendahl, a Protestant scholar, former dean of Harvard Divinity School, bishop of Stockholm, Sweden, and a pioneer of Jewish-Christian dialogue, wrote of him, "Samuel Sandmel was a gift of God to both Jews and Christians. It was given to him to help change the climate and even the agenda of Jewish-Christian conversations."[6] Many Jews involved in

---

[4] Hebrew Union College, founded by Isaac Mayer Wise in 1875, and the Jewish Institute of Religion, founded by Stephen S. Wise (no relation) in 1922, merged in 1950.

[5] In addition to his scholarship, he published a novel, and his short story "The Colleagues of Mr. Chips" was included in *The Best American Short Stories 1961*, edited by Martha Foley and David Burnett (Boston: Houghton Mifflin, 1961. The most complete bibliography of his work can be found in *Nourished with Peace: Studies in Hellenistic Judaism in Memory of Samuel Sandmel*, edited by Frederick E. Greenspahn, Earle Hilgert, and Burton L. Mack (Chico, CA: Scholars Press, 1984), 221–237.

[6] "A Friend and His Philo-Connection," in *Nourished with Peace*, 13.

Jewish-Christian dialogue concentrate on pointing out those aspects of Christian texts and Christian theology that lie at the heart of the Jewish-Christian tragedy. My father did not shy away from this, but he was equally committed to teaching Jews how to approach Christianity with respect. *A Jewish Understanding of the New Testament* marks his first major effort in this regard and, with two other books, written primarily for a popular audience, comprise a kind of trilogy: this book, *We Jews and Jesus* (1965, 1973), and *We Jews and You Christians* (1967).

To the best of my knowledge, *A Jewish Understanding of the New Testament,* the third edition of which was published by SkyLight Paths Publishing in 2005, remains the only book written by a Jew about the New Testament. This was true in 1956 when the book was first published, it was true in 1974 when my father noted this fact in the introduction to an augmented edition of the book, and it remains true today. Jews have written extensively on Jesus, Paul, Christianity, and on aspects or parts of the New Testament, but no other Jew has written a book on the New Testament itself.

As the title suggests, *We Jews and You Christians* was written for a Christian audience in an effort "to give an answer to a question very often put to me by Christians: What is the attitude of you Jews to us?"[7] The book concludes with a remarkable and, I believe, largely overlooked "Proposed Declaration: 'The Synagogue and the Christian People'" that in many ways presages "Dabru Emet." That two of these books are written primarily for Jews and one primarily for Christians is a bit artificial; in all three my father addresses both Jews and Christians and, indeed, both Jews and Christians have read all three books and learned from them. A fourth book, *The Genius of Paul,* although more academic than the other three, deserves mention because my father did think that one could write about Paul, unlike Jesus, since some of Paul's own writings have survived.

This book, *We Jews and Jesus,* was written "for those thoughtful Jewish people who seek to arrive at a calm and balanced under-

---

[7] *We Jews and You Christians,* 1.

standing of where Jews can reasonably stand with respect to Jesus."[8] It was published in the same year as Nostra Aetate, that brief document of the Second Vatican Council that addresses the issue of how the Roman Catholic Church views non-Christian religions. Primary among the document's affirmations are that Jesus, Mary, the Apostles and many of the early disciples were Jewish; that neither all the Jews of Jesus's days, nor Jews of subsequent ages should be held responsible for the death of Jesus; and that God's covenant with the Jewish people described in scripture is irrevocable. While not the first or the only Christian statement to make these claims, because of the prestige of the Vatican and the size of the Roman Catholic Church, Nostra Aetate is by far the best known and the most significant. If there is one moment that marks the radical shift in the relationship between Christians and Jews in the post-Holocaust era, it is the publication of Nostra Aetate. My father discusses the impending promulgation of this document in the final section of this book.

The decades after World War II saw other significant changes that influenced Jewish interest in Jesus. As Christians came more and more to acknowledge, and even to celebrate, the Jewishness of Jesus, Jews, perhaps in response, became more interested in learning about this important Jew. The roots of this trend go back to the nineteenth century, with Jewish scholars such as Heinrich Graetz (1817–1891) and Abraham Geiger (1810–1874), as well as early twentieth-century scholars like Joseph Klausner (1874–1958) and Claude G. Montefiore (1858–1938). However, Jewish interest in the historical Jesus mushroomed after the Holocaust with the emergence of the Jewish-Christian dialogue movement, advances in historical Jesus scholarship, and increasing popular attention to this scholarship—driven in part by archaeology finds in the land of Israel in general and the discovery of the Dead Sea Scrolls in particular.

I think it is fair to say that there has been a symbiotic relationship between the dialogue movement and scholarship on

---

[8] *We Jews and Jesus*, xv.

Judaism and Christianity in antiquity. As relations between Jews and Christians have improved, the willingness and even the ability of scholars to reconsider aspects of scholarship that had been distorted by the unquestioned negative attitudes toward Jews and Judaism have led to a more sophisticated and historically nuanced image of the formative centuries of both Christianity and Rabbinic Judaism. This in turn has provided those involved in the dialogue with new models for exploring the relationship between the two traditions.

For example, traditionally the Church presented the Judaism of the time of Jesus as monolithic, legalistic, and oppressive. Jesus came to free his downtrodden people from the yoke of a petrified religion overseen by a corrupt priesthood. In this construction, Jesus the liberator is seen in opposition to the Judaism of his day. This image of the origins of Christianity mirrored the evaluation of Judaism that was part of the Church's theology. Jesus and the Church represented the good and the right; Judaism and the Jews represented the opposite. Today, most Christians (and Jews) accept the scholarly consensus that the Judaism of Jesus's day was vibrant and varied and that most Jews were fiercely loyal to their people and their tradition. Jesus is now understood to have been one of these loyal Jews, and to be understood correctly Jesus must be seen within, rather than opposed to, the Judaism of his day.

My father's work, both his more popular writings, such as this volume, and his academic works, influenced a generation of both scholars and Jewish and Christian clergy.

It is certainly legitimate to ask how well a book such as this holds up after more than forty years. On the one hand, during that time, many Jews have written about Jesus. Among those more contemporary scholars not treated in *We Jews and Jesus* are David Flusser (1917–2000), Jacob Neusner (1932–), Paula Fredriksen (1951–), and Irving Greenberg (1933–). The works of these scholars, and many others, have added to the complexity of the Jewish views of Jesus. One area that my father did not address was the treatment of Jesus in literature by Jews (with the exception of reference in a footnote to the novels of Sholom

Asch), or in art, such as the works of Marc Chagall, or in film. He limited his examination to what could be found in traditional Jewish religious literature and in modern scholarship, his primary areas of scholarly expertise.

Notwithstanding the advances in scholarship since it was first published, *We Jews and Jesus* remains an eminently accessible and useful introduction, not just to Jewish views of Jesus through history but also to historical Jesus scholarship. Those who wish to read further are directed both to the bibliography that was part of the original text of the book (beginning on page 154), and to my own selected bibliography (beginning on page xiv) that refers to many more of the significant works published over the last forty years.

Updated Bibliography to the New Edition

Ben Chorin, Shalom. "The Image of Jesus in Modern Judaism." *Journal of Ecumenical Studies* 11 (1974): 401–430.

Berlin, George L. *Defending the Faith: Nineteenth-Century American Jewish Writings on Christianity and Jesus.* SUNY series in religious studies. Albany: State University of New York Press, 1989.

Brumberg-Kraus, Jonathan. "A Jewish Ideological Perspective on the Study of Christian Scripture." *Jewish Social Studies* N.S. 4:1 (1997): 121–152.

Catchpole, David R. *The Trial of Jesus: A Study in the Gospels and Jewish Historiography from 1770 to the Present Day.* Studia post-Biblica. v. 18. Leiden: Brill Academic Publishers, 1997.

Flusser, David. *Jesus.* Translated by Walls, R. New York: Herder and Herder, 1969.

Fredriksen, Paula. *From Jesus to Christ: The Origins of the New Testament Images of Jesus.* New Haven: Yale University Press, 2000.

Goldstein, Morris. *Jesus in the Jewish Tradition.* New York: Macmillan, 1950.

Greenberg, Irving. *For the Sake of Heaven and Earth: The New Encounter between Judaism and Christianity.* Philadelphia: Jewish Publication Society of America, 2004.

Heschel, Susannah. "Jesus as a Theological Transvestite." In *Judaism Since Gender,* ed. Miriam Peskowitz and Laura Levitt. New York: Routledge, 1997.

Heschel, Susannah, *Abraham Geiger and the Jewish Jesus.* Chicago: University of Chicago Press, 1998.

Jacob, Walter. *Christianity through Jewish Eyes: The Quest for Common Ground.* New York: KTAV Publishers, 1974.

Lapide, Pinchas. *Israelis, Jews and Jesus.* Translated by P. Heinegg. Garden City: Doubleday, 1979.

Lauterbach, Jacob. "Jesus in the Talmud." In *Rabbinic Essays,* 473–570. New York: KTAV Publishers, 1973.

Maccoby, Hyam. *Revolution in Judaea: Jesus and the Jewish Resistance.* New York: Taplinger Publishing, 1981.

Neusner, Jacob. *A Rabbi Talks with Jesus: An Intermillennial, Interfaith Exchange.* New York: Doubleday, 1993.

Sandmel, Samuel. "The Jewish Scholar and Early Christianity." In *The Seventy-fifth Anniversary Volume of the Jewish Quarterly Review,* ed. Abraham A. Newman and Solomon Zeitlin, 473–481. New York: KTAV Publishers, 1967.

Sandmel, Samuel. *A Jewish Understanding of the New Testament.* Woodstock, VT: Skylight Paths Publishing, 2005.

Schonfield, Hugh. *The Passover Plot: A New Interpretation of the Life and Death of Jesus.* New York: Geis, 1998.

Vermes, Geza. *Jesus the Jew: A Historian's Reading of the Gospels.* Minneapolis: Augsburg Fortress Publishers, 1981.

Weaver, Walter P. *The Historical Jesus in the Twentieth Century, 1900–1950.* Harrisburg: Trinity International Press, 1999.

Weiss-Rosmarin, Trude. *Jewish Expressions on Jesus: An Anthology.* New York: KTAV Publishers, 1977.

Preface to the 1965 Edition

I have written this little book for those thoughtful Jewish people who seek to arrive at a calm and balanced understanding of where Jews can reasonably stand with respect to Jesus. For the impulsive or intuitive, an essay rather than a book would suffice. Such essays, competently written in the last half-century a great number of times by a great number of able rabbis, normally make two brief points. The first of these is that those Christian views which regard Jesus as more than a man are inconsistent with Judaism and uncongenial to Jews; this view often focuses on the "Christian Christ." The second is that those virtues ascribed to Jesus the man, the "Jewish Jesus," are characteristic Jewish virtues, expressed in Judaism and integrally a part of it. Such a Jewish Jesus may well have been a good and great man—a prophet, a rabbi, or a patriotic leader—but he was not better or greater, say these writings, than other great Jews.

These two points probably reflect responsibly the essence of what there is to be said, but this usually constitutes merely a skeleton without the flesh of detail. What I have tried to do is to treat the complex question with what I hope is a little more profundity.

I have tried also to treat it with that respect which I believe the question can and should have. At times the question has been asked in a way that has tended to deprive it of respect. For example, Jews have asked fellow Jews in a belligerent or scolding way if it is not time for Jews to abstain from withholding from Jesus certain accolades for what the questioners have assumed that he has accomplished. Sometimes the issue has been raised in the form of a dramatic statement by a Jew to other Jews. On the other hand, at the end of the eighteenth century a German Jew proposed to Christians that he and some of his contemporaries were prepared to concede a uniqueness to the man Jesus, and the offended reply to him was to the effect that Christians did not regard Jesus as merely a man. When the question has been raised in an unfortunate way by a Jew, the answers, especially from other Jews, have often partaken of the unfortunate.

Even the calm and judicious essays by Jews have frequently lacked two elements that I have tried to supply here. The first of these is a sense of the scope of the problem. It is not, as some think, a problem new to our time; for almost two hundred years a host of Jews have addressed themselves to it. I do not try to reflect all of the Jewish opinions, for many are repetitious of each other, but I do try to cite some of the major motifs of Jewish writings on the subject so that the reader can see, or at least glimpse, the earnestness with which Jews have approached the question. Second, on the conviction that an informed opinion can be superior to an uninformed one, I have devoted the major part of this book to reproducing some of the concerns and the conclusions of technical scholars, both Christians and Jews. Chapter 4 is by design a rather long, yet telescoped, account of the march of Gospel scholarship in the past 175 years. In writing that chapter, I had to make the choice of whether to pursue a series of topics or whether to follow a chronological account. I have chosen the latter course because it seems to me the best way to bring matters up to our own time and thus to provide the background of my own approach. For some readers this chronological sequence may make the going a little hard, especially since I interrupt the account to consider, and explain, some relevant topics. For example, it is in that chapter that I digress to discuss the different bodies of data about Judaism in the age of Jesus, the rabbinic on the one hand and the writings in Greek on the other hand. In that chapter, too, I discuss a question often put to me by Jews, to the effect that perhaps there never was a Jesus. To reflect for the general reader what scholars have written in technical books poses for the interpreter the acute problem of conveying clarity while at the same time dealing responsibly with the scholarship he is citing. I have earnestly tried to accomplish this. I can only say that the reader who wants to know *why* Jews think as they do about Jesus, as distinct from the easier question, *what* do Jews think, might find a second reading of Chapter 4 more rewarding than the first.

More specifically, I have tried to provide a small book that Jewish parents, after they themselves have read it, might put into the hands of college-age students. It has been my observation that a Jewish youngster, away from home and sharing in the great adventure of higher education with fellow students who are Christians, could benefit from such an endeavor. Yet even with this audience in mind, the inevitable questions of how much to include, and what could be omitted, are not solved here any more than they are in my deliberately selective work.

I have tried to write straightforwardly. I am reconciled in advance to the possibility that what I say may offend some Christians who read this book. But the intention with which I set forth the ensuing views, and the manner in which I present them, I hope cannot possibly be misconstrued. I have asked two Christian scholars, one a Protestant, Morton S. Enslin, and the other a Roman Catholic priest, Father John L. Mackenzie, to read this book in manuscript to forfend against such involuntary offensiveness. I am responsible for this book, not they. But I am in great debt to them. Professor Enslin in particular made many candid comments and suggestions, and these have aided me greatly. I asked the help of these scholars because I respect the question, which is the purpose of this book, and because it was, and is, my conviction that the ties of friendship and of mutual scholarly endeavor between us made it seem a highly desirable step, indeed quite a natural one, in the context of the way in which biblical scholarship is practiced today.

I have tried not to stray from the particular topic into those broader matters which I have treated in *A Jewish Understanding of the New Testament* and in *Judaism and Christianity*. Some of what I have written there is repeated here; that has been unavoidable. But my focus here is quite different, and most of what I have here written is not found there.

Finally I record my deep gratitude to Mrs. Helen Lederer and Mrs. Rissa Alex for their help in transferring a penciled manuscript into a typescript. Rabbi Joseph Karasick, academic coordinator of the Cincinnati School of the Hebrew Union College–Jewish

Institute of Religion, and the Reverend Mr. Hugh Haggard, a graduate student, have scrutinized the manuscript for me, and Mr. Haggard has checked the bibliographic details and compiled the index. My secretary, Mrs. Sam November, has assisted in countless, and matchless, ways. My wife desisted from her own writing projects to help in matters of style; I record here, inadequately, my gratitude to her.

We
Jews
and
Jesus

CHAPTER 1 · Introduction

In the past one hundred and fifty years there has taken place what amounts to a reversal of eighteen centuries of Jewish and Christian attitudes toward each other. This reversal, which is part of other tremendous upheavals in the thought and life of Western man, is by no means complete, nor is it everywhere uniform. Indeed, the older attitudes have abided unchanged in substantial segments of both traditions. It is nevertheless correct to speak of the historic animosities as having been eased, and of having been replaced by both knowledge and a disposition toward genuine understanding. There exists now a greater array of elements that bind the two traditions together than formerly could be marshaled to maintain the antagonisms and misunderstandings.

In this context of a reversal of historic attitudes, it is appropriate to examine one specific item, a Jewish attitude toward Jesus. This book is an inquiry into that subject. The inquiry falls into three natural divisions. First, I give a résumé of pre-modern Jewish approaches. Second, I give what seems to me to be a reasoned and reasonable approach by a modern Jew, presented in the light of the scholarship of the last century and a half as pursued by Christians and Jews. Thereafter I make some comments on the implications of that approach to Christian-Jewish relations.

I must be straightforward in saying that my approach is partisan; it is Jewish and not neutral. At the same time I am something of a scholar, and that implies, if not neutrality, at least an effort toward objectivity. Indeed, the reader who may expect an easy essay which is primarily interpretive will be disappointed to find that this book is largely expository, a setting forth of information and of facts, and even of acknowledgments of places where we are without facts. Since such an exposition ought to be detached and objective, I have tried to be faithful to these requirements. Accordingly, I shall be treating dispassionately materials about which people have felt great passion and ardor. There is the danger that some Christians may mistakenly confuse academic dispassion with disdain; this could especially be the case among those Christians for whom the serious research into Christian origins is a new adventure and who are therefore unacquainted with the history of the Protestant Gospel scholarship which I, a rabbi, learned from my Protestant teachers. I own to being influenced in my attitude to Christianity by warm sympathy for it, and even concern and respect. Perhaps these latter seem obscured in, and even to disappear from, some of the ensuing pages, for two reasons beyond scholarly detachment.

The first reason is that as I am not a Christian, my Jewish partisanship may manifest itself even more than I am aware. I strive for an honest and just description and evaluation, but I know that an outsider to any tradition constantly runs the risk of misunderstanding, or falling short of understanding, a tradition not innately his own. Since I see many examples of this blemish in what Christians have written about Judaism, I must assume that it is to some degree inescapable; I can only try to escape it as much as possible.

The second reason for the possibility of some distortion in my presentation is that the history of Christendom is marred by many chapters that are ugly. There are more such chapters relating to events entirely within Christianity than between Christianity and Judaism. If I mention the Crusades, the crusade against the Albigensian heretics, and the religious wars and persecutions after the Protestant Reformation, then I am here only echoing the lament of modern Christian historians in their exposition and interpretation of the Christian history. As to Christians and Jews, however, there is the risk to be run that to recall the persecutions in Europe centuries ago can tend to revive, among some people today, the hostility that ought not to be revived. He who calls it to mind can even falsely seem to share in that hostility. Let me state that I do not hold, and it does not seem reasonable to me to hold, my American Christian neighbor responsible for what Christians did to my Jewish forebears long ago in Europe. The twofold purpose of hearkening back to those dismal and unfortunate events is, first, to clarify certain matters and issues, and, second, and more importantly, for us to understand by the contrast between the present and the past how far we have moved. I believe that if Christians and Jews are genuinely to understand each other they must first face such facts and thereafter proceed to understand the facts, and each other.

Yet my topic is not Christianity and Judaism, but rather "We Jews and Jesus." Only where the restricted topic requires it have I touched on or entered into the broader questions, for those could and should comprise a book in itself.

In addition to my being Jewish, I am a product of the intellectual stream of modern times. My spiritual legacy from the past, like that of other American Jews, includes, in addition to Judaism, Greece and Rome, the Protestant Reformation, Humanism, the French Revolution, Darwin and Freud, and, for that matter, Shakespeare and Beethoven and Puccini.

All these factors are involved in how I think, and what I think. Yet they are involved also in how I feel. Since to all things I react in some measure with the heart, obviously in this matter of Jesus and us Jews I do so too. So do most Jews. A complete psychological syndrome exists, and its existence ought to be acknowledged and its nature described—even though its gravity defies accurate assessment. The "problem" of Jesus for modern Jews is not only religious and psychological, but it is also cultural and sociological. It is especially rooted in matters of history, in matters of inherited folklore, and in what partakes of folk experience and folk wisdom, even in modern and cosmopolitan situations.

A first item involves an inescapable necessity. Christians and Jews need to recognize that Christianity and Judaism until the modern age—and I will presently define what I mean by the modern age—have felt about each other that they were mutually exclusive, reciprocally contradictory of each other, and that the one was true and the other false.

Though in the Middle Ages an occasional eminent Jewish voice, a Judah Ha-Levi or a Joseph Albo, conceded that certain values existed in Christian practice and thought, by and large the usual attitudes of the two religions to each other were dominated by a sense of grievances. From the Christian side, a large number of passages in Christian Scripture fastened on Jews the direct responsibility for the death of Jesus and for the persecution of the early Church. In the New Testament, in passages other than those dealing with the responsibility of the crucifixion, Jews are frequently depicted as hypocrites in relationship to merits implicitly conceded by New Testament writers to inhere in Judaism. Such passages suggest or state that Christians are capable of so distinguishing between mere formal externals and the heart of religious aspirations as to be free from hypocrisy.

On still another level, the contention is found in the New Testament that Judaism is wrong in principle. This contention takes the form of asserting that the Law found in the Five Books of Moses is not only incapable of bringing men to righteousness, but that the Law is the veritable obstacle to the achievement of it. An abundance of passages, especially in the Epistles of Paul, attribute to the Law the character of a "dispensation of death," while the Christian "Gospel" is by contrast that which brings life. The Law of Moses is depicted as a deficient and outmoded instrument for attaining righteousness, and it is constantly regarded in the Epistles as superseded, and hence is abrogated. A new covenant, between God and the Christians, replaces and supplants the old covenant between God and the Jews; the "promises" of

God's favor and guidance contained in the Jewish Scripture, so the Christian writings tell us, are still valid, but it is Christians to whom and for whom the promises are henceforth to be effectuated, and the Jews have lost to the Christians their erstwhile priority and favored position in the economy of God's love and grace. The Jews, so it is averred, had the opportunity to continue in God's favor, but because of their blindness about Jesus, they are no longer able to share in God's blessings through the medium of their inherited Judaism, but can do so only through Christianity. They were invited, and still are, to become Christians and thus participate in the divine blessings, and it is a Christian grievance that Jews have ordinarily rejected the invitation. It is a Christian grievance that the Christian way is so palpably superior to the Jewish way that Jews ought not to have been so stubborn in failing to discern the superiority; instead Jews have responded with hostility and even with scorn. It is a Christian grievance that it was Gentiles who responded affirmatively to the Christian propositions, and that the Jews, who might reasonably have been even more prone to respond affirmatively, did not do so, and instead obdurately rejected, and malevolently tried to refute, the Christian propositions, thereby making the task of Christians all the more arduous. Christians have made overtures to Jews throughout the ages to enter the Church, but the bulk of Jews have not done so. To sum up, it is a Christian grievance that Christianity is true, and it is noble, and it is fine, but Jews have denied the truth, and they have regarded Christians as the reverse of noble and fine.

The Jewish grievance exists on several levels. Why should Christians have wanted them to concede as true that which they did not believe was true? How could Christians have the temerity to asperse the divine Laws of Moses, and to proceed to regard them as abrogated? How could Christians regard Jesus as divine in the light of his crucifixion, and at the same time blame Jews, mere men, for the death of a divine being? How could Christians so extend the blame for the death of Jesus that Jews, born centuries later and thousands of miles away, and despite obvious innocence, still were held responsible and guilty? How could a religious system that accused Jews of hypocrisy itself escape that charge when, pretending to kindliness, it limited Jews economically and politically, herded them into ghettoes, and compelled them to wear badges to identify them as unworthy outsiders? How could Christians apotheosize a "prince of peace," in the light of the countless wars of Christendom? What boast could Christians properly make of the alleged superiority of Christianity in view of the demonstrable failure of Christian civilization to live, at least in its relations with Jews, on even a minimum standard of religious principles?

The Jewish grievance is compounded of these and other elements; and if the Middle Ages had not come to an end, these particular grievances could and would still abide. The fact is that the Protestant Reformation, the age of mercantilism, and the Industrial Revolution forced a divided Christendom into religious toleration for the sake of peace among the denominations, and progressively, though often reluctantly, the same toleration gradually was extended to include Jews. The "Jew-badge," imposed by Christians, disappeared (to be revived by the Nazi Germans); the compulsory ghetto was dissolved; and in Western lands Jews were at last enfranchised to participate in some fullness of the economic, political, and cultural life. Certain social limitations existed, and also economic counterparts. In Germany, in the early nineteenth century, Jews were still without the rights of citizenship, and entry into the professions was denied them except after conversion to Christianity. It is a noteworthy fact that Jews had resisted conversion, even forced conversion, in the Middle Ages, despite persecutions and expulsions. But in early nineteenth-century Germany, so eager were many Jews for acceptance, and so relatively unimportant did conversion appear, that many Jews became baptized; the deist attack on religion had made affiliation, whether to Judaism or to Christianity, so unimportant to these people that they took the step. To other Jews in Germany, this apostasy was shocking on many levels. In the first place, it represented a disloyalty to the Jewish people comparable to treason, for the apostate not only abandoned his ancestral faith but allied himself to the faith of the foe, the persecutor. In the second place, such conversions represented convenience rather than conviction, as was well attested by the poet Heinrich Heine and his ironic comments about his own conversion to Christianity, with the consequence that Jews did not credit such converts with sincerity and, indeed, ordinarily still do not. If perhaps this doubt about sincerity of converts was largely a matter of mere arrogance, a matter of wondering how one could abandon the manifest truth, Judaism, for transparent error, Christianity, the doubt underwent, among early nineteenth-century German Jews, a certain change in its character. It became, in an age and among people of extreme sophistication and irreligion, a matter of wondering how a person emancipated from Judaism could embrace what seemed to Jews in these "enlightened" circles an even more extreme irrationalism.

More generally, if one can trespass into a psychiatric diagnosis, Jews have reacted instinctively away from the apostate not merely out of considerations of group loyalty but out of the fear of what the former member of their group might turn and do to them. Not only has Jewish folklore, stemming from the Middle Ages, transmitted with some high measure of accuracy a vivid and reliable summary of the evil which the lies of apostates caused to Jews on historic occasions, but converts from Judaism to Christianity have often been motivated less by the attraction of Christianity than by the disabilities of being Jewish. Since the apostate rejects his former faith, he scarcely does so out of love; and if his rejection comes out of hate, then his former coreligionists could have reason to fear his hate, if by chance they lived in a situation in which that sort of hate could lead to overt acts against them.

The Jewish grievance at what apostates have caused Jews to suffer still involves Jews in contradictions. A Jew, for example, can feel unreserved love and affection for a "born" Christian, and still be unable to see any affirmative qualities in a Jewish convert to Christianity. Christians have so failed to understand the Jewish instinct about apostates that still today they ordinarily entrust to former Jews the task of converting Jews to Christianity, possibly on the basis that the example might persuade, or that the apostate possesses the requisite knowledge for effective proselytizing. I do not hesitate to advise Christians that they can make no worse choice than to appoint a Jewish apostate to the chore of converting us Jews.

The fact is that Jews look askance not only at conversion from Judaism, but also (this I record with regret) at conversion to Judaism. Some of the reasons are the same, but some are different and not altogether admirable; within the latter sphere is an instinctive borrowing from "racism" and a consequent denial that one can be a Jew except by birth. Those Jews who look askance at conversion to Judaism have had more to look at in recent years.

The relevancy of these comments can be the clearer if we proceed to a plain statement. The practices of Christianity, and its literature, do not have for a Jew (whether he is faithful or faithless to his Judaism) those values which they have for a Christian. I have in mind the Gospels in particular. Yet if I am to be fully understood by Christian readers, I must lead into this subject in a roundabout way.

The impartial reader of the account of the early years of Jacob in Genesis can see that it is the story of the likeable rogue; the total story deals with the transformation of a character from early misdeeds into later righteousness.[1] In the early years Jacob twice cheats his brother Esau, first for the *bekora,* the rights of the first born, and second, for the *beraka,* the blessing of their father Isaac. To the impartial reader, Jacob is clearly the aggressor and Esau clearly the victim. Yet in Jewish scriptural interpretation, it is normal to regard Esau as the evil one and Jacob as the righteous one. That is to say, prepossession can so dominate the reader of a document that the document can often mean whatever the prepossessor consciously or unconsciously intends. There exists what psychologists call an "apperceptive mass," an aggregate of antecedent opinions and feelings which shape the response of a person to what he newly encounters. (The scholar achieves his objectivity only to the extent that he takes fullest account of his own apperceptive mass.)

The rites, and ceremonies, and beliefs of traditions not our own can seem strange, and even ridiculous, while our own can seem true and beautiful and reasonable. If we are students of anthro-

pology, then we are motivated to try to understand rites, ceremonies, and beliefs within the context of the given religion. If we
do not make this effort, then we can be misled into mere partisanship. If we are Jews, we can deride holy water, and the wafer and
the wine; if we are Christians, we can deride the abstinence from
pork and shellfish, or the substituting of matzo for bread during
Passover.

One motif which Jews and Christians have shared is a blind
hatred of pagan religion. The Jewish and Christian Scriptures,
and subsequent literatures, are replete with denunciations of
paganism. I know of no passage in the ancient writings that makes
any effort toward a sympathetic understanding of that expression
of the human longing.

Yet the animosity toward paganism, toward outsiders, is mild
compared to that exhibited toward heretics. The heretic is not an
outsider, but part and parcel of the tradition, and hence is charge-
able with wilful rejection of the truth, while the pagan may possibly be excused because of his unwitting ignorance.

In the apperceptive mass of the usual Jew and Christian in the
Middle Ages, to each the other partook of the character both of
the pagan and the heretic, and the respective rites, ceremonies,
and beliefs were assessed on that basis. Two different apperceptive masses governed the assessment even of those matters held
in common; Christians and Jews held in common what Christians
called the Old Testament and Jews called The Bible, yet they
neither read it nor understood it in the same way.

The Christians read the Gospels in the light of a Christian
apperceptive mass. Jesus not only is the protagonist in the Gospels, but to the Christian reader he is so sublime in his character
and so all-encompassing in his knowledge and religious sensitivity
that the reader never deviates from an affirmative assessment or
some sense of identification with him. The Jewish reader, on the
other hand, is governed by the instinct to refute what the Gospels
say, to make the opponents of Jesus the protagonists, and to discover in himself a constantly renewed astonishment that such
material could ever be believed, or even seem to be edifying. The
first book of consequence on the Gospels written from a Jewish

viewpoint was "Faith Strengthened," by Isaak Troki,[2] published in Hebrew in 1593; it was translated into many languages, the English edition being published in 1851. It was a formidable assault on the credibility of the Gospels as entities; in addition, it dealt with those countless details in the Gospels which were destined to preoccupy Christian scholars when scientific scholarship arose in the end of the eighteenth century. Troki displays the approach of the medieval person, in that the urge to refute was stronger than the impulse to understand. While the usual medieval Jew did not possess any real knowledge of the contents of the Gospels, he was preconditioned, especially by persecution, to the basic attitude which Troki exhibits.

Another book, a very ancient work, *Toledot Jeshu*, "The History of Jesus," was to be found occasionally among Jews. This Aramaic work, possibly as old as the sixth century, was derived both from earlier Jewish skepticism about Jesus and from the Gospels themselves, the Gospel details fitting into the work by the simple mechanism of turning evil into good and good into evil. In this work, Jesus is the illegitimate son of Mary and Joseph, the latter having seduced her; her husband, Johanan, disowned her and fled to Babylon. *Toledot Jeshu* is quite an unedifying work and in its tone is a counterpart of Christian disparagements of Judaism. Never broadly circulated or read, its lamentable contents were nevertheless known to Jews who never heard of the book; the alleged illegitimacy of Jesus, a retort to the virgin birth, was widely held by Jews of the Middle Ages. They customarily referred to Jesus by the Hebrew word *talui*, "the hanged one," and as Jews moved about and changed pronunciation, the two consonants remained unchanged, but the vowels underwent permutation and the resultant forms have been "tola," or "toyla," or the like.

This negative apperceptive mass abided sturdily among Jews as long as the Middle Ages abided. But whereas in the Westerner's study of history the Middle Ages are regarded as ended at least by the time of the French Revolution, for Jews in Eastern Europe medievalism abided literally into our time. The Jewish masses of

Poland, Russia, and Rumania never experienced the "rights of man," and only a small handful of them were touched by that East European reflection of Western Enlightenment called the "Haskala." Whereas in Western Europe the great transition in the lot of Jews occurred at the end of the eighteenth and the beginning of the nineteenth centuries, for my parents, born in Eastern Europe, it was delayed until the twentieth century, and it was achieved by crossing the ocean.

American Jews like me have encountered in my day replicas of the intellectual challenges encountered by German and French Jews well over a century ago, when they were released from a self-contained Jewish environment and exposed to the cultural ideas of the milieu at large. The challenge is comparable, but the environments are totally different, for we American Jews have never had to struggle for political rights, having been born into a relatively high measure of religious toleration, and we have enjoyed an unprecedented high peace and harmony with our Christian neighbors. One need not gloss over the minor recurrences of anti-Jewish sentiments in the United States, yet these are so minor that one does not exaggerate when he says that never in the Diaspora has a Jewish community lived in so favorable a situation. To the extent that the modern scene had urged that religious toleration replace intolerance, and mutual respect replace disparagement, it has been inescapable that Jews rethink and revise the inherited apperceptive mass.

To do so, whether in Germany in the early part of the nineteenth century, or in the United States by people of my background in the twentieth century, has meant to trespass into untraditionalism through an intellectual appreciation of other traditions. To do so has meant to expose oneself to a misunderstanding among some segments of one's own Jewish people, for to such segments it has seemed impossible for one and the same person to combine in himself an unswerving loyalty to Judaism and a willingness seriously to inquire into Christianity. Enlightenment has not permeated Jews completely any more than it has Christianity. Let me simply restate then my full Jewish loyalty.

In speaking of the multiple upheavals in politics, economics, and learning that took place at the close of the eighteenth and the beginning of the nineteenth centuries, it is necessary to comment on a notable factor which unconsciously gave a sanction to Jews of that time to rethink their attitude toward Jesus. I have described the historic attitude of Jews as negative, a compound of skepticism and disparagement. The age of deism brought about the curious development that circles that were previously Christian now created their own skepticism and disparagement. A Western Jew could find support for his negativism about Christianity from the philosophical atmosphere of that age.

Much of the eighteenth-century deist disparagement of the historicity of the Gospels was intuitive rather than learned. It was a denial of the Gospel miracles, rather than a judicious scholarly appraisal of the Gospel materials. It served the important purpose of compelling loyal Christians into a new depth of scholarship, a scholarship in which solid learning, objective and accurate, was to replace the merely doctrinal conclusions of the past.

When, in the eighteenth century, the deists had distinguished between natural and revealed religion, and had demanded that advocates of a revealed religion must produce "historical evidences," Christian partisans were not backward in producing works which attempted to justify Christian claims through historical research rather than faith alone. As a by-product, Christian scholars, giving a new emphasis to historical research, embarked on what has been called the "quest for the historical Jesus." This began and flourished in Germany, and it was also in Germany that the Enlightenment had penetrated among Jews. The canons of objective, thorough scholarship thus entered into Jewish learning as well; the "Science of Judaism" (*Die Wissenschaft des Judentums*) is the name given to this new Jewish scholarship. Accordingly, strict objectivity in study became as much a requirement for Jews as for other scholars, with the result that the one-sidedness of an Isaak Troki was necessarily abandoned. The ideal of these Christian scholars was to describe exactly who and what Jesus was; in such an effort Jewish scholars could join. And since Jesus was a Jew, an effort to recover the

Jesus of history carried with it the need to try to recover, just as objectively, the Judaism of the age of Jesus. For this latter, Jewish scholars were to serve in a way often denied to Christians, for reasons we shall see. But, more to the point, Jewish historians of the nineteenth century differed from those of earlier times in that they did not pretend that Christianity did not exist, and they did not shun the obligation, in depicting the history of Jews in the Graeco-Roman period, to include Jesus and early Christianity in their study. In Eastern Europe broadly, and in Western Europe sporadically, the age-old attitudes still abided; but Jewish scholars had committed themselves to the goal of full historical truth.

I have spoken of Troki's list of discordant details in the Gospels; I have alluded to a new and scientific mode of study. What the new study required was that scholars face squarely the existence of real problems, rather than gloss over them, or distort them—face squarely all the problems, the disconcerting as well as the trivial. The achievements of nineteenth-century New Testament scholars were tremendous.

But their scholarship was not disinterested; it had the motive of using the tools of learning so as to isolate the figure of Jesus, a historical person, non-miraculous in character, whose endowments and accomplishments entitled him to a continued respect, and whose teachings, when the authentic would have been winnowed out of the mass of the inauthentic, could still have a validity for modern man. Christian scholars sought for the Jesus of history so as to have a basis for a continued Christianity; Jewish scholars inquired into who Jesus was in order to understand that phenomenon called Christianity, and to see more clearly the nature of Judaism in the age of Jesus.

The approach of the Jew of today to Jesus must take into account the following factors. First, what has traditional Christianity thought of him? Second, what does modern scientific scholarship tell about him? Third, what have modern Jewish scholars told us of him as far as their historical studies disclose? Fourth, what are the characteristics of Judaism, and how does Jesus fit into both our inherited Judaism and into the Judaism of today?

Notes

1. I have given a rather full exposition in my book, *The Hebrew Scriptures,* pp. 361ff.

2. Troki was a Karaite, a sect which arose in the eighth century. The Karaites rejected the rabbinic law and literature, and reverted to Scripture itself. The word Karaite means "Biblist." Today the Karaites number only a few thousand, where once they were exceedingly numerous.

CHAPTER 2 · Early Christianity and Its Jewish Background

What knowledge we have about Jesus comes only from the New Testament. He went unmentioned in the surviving Jewish [1] and pagan literature of his time. Passages about him in the ancient rabbinic literature are sometimes cited as if they reflect knowledge of him independent of the New Testament; I agree with that majority of students who view these passages rather as derivative from, or reflective of, the New Testament materials and of Christian tradition. The historian Josephus (A.D. 37–105) gave a paragraph about John the Baptist, a contemporary whom the Gospels bring into relationship with Jesus; there is no reason to discount the reliability of the paragraph. There is also found in *Antiquities of the Jews*, XVIII, III, 4, the following paragraph: "There was about this time Jesus, a wise man, if it is right to call him man, for he was a doer of wonderful works, a teacher of such men as receive the truth with pleasure. He drew over to him both many of the Jews and many of the Gentiles. He was Christ. And when Pilate, at the suggestion of the principal men among us, had condemned him to the cross, those that loved at the first did not forsake him, for he appeared to them alive again the third day, as the divine prophets had foretold these and myriad other wonderful things concerning him. The tribe of Christians, so named for him, are not extinct to this day."

For a Jew so to have written is a little surprising. What is even more surprising is that, although Church fathers quoted Josephus frequently, and this paragraph would have suited their purposes admirably, yet they never quoted it. Most scholars believe the passage is entirely an interpolation; a few believe that it is a replacement, or rewriting, of an authentic paragraph now beyond recovery; only an infinitesimal number of scholars attribute authenticity to the passage. To conclude that Josephus did not mention Jesus underscores what was said above, that we know about him only what the New Testament tells us.

The sum total of what the New Testament tells us is notably small. There are mentions of Jesus in virtually all twenty-seven books of the New Testament. The principal materials are the four Gospels. Each is named for the presumed author: Matthew, Mark, Luke, and John. The first three Gospels overlap greatly in contents; almost all of Mark is found in both Matthew and Luke, and we must bear this in mind in justifying the contention that the sum total is small. Moreover, Matthew and Luke contain duplicating material.[2] This indicates again how relatively small the total body of material is.

Matthew and Luke each has a small amount of material not duplicated in any other of the Gospels. John is different in manner and content from the other three. John contains elaborate and frequent soliloquies, and a relative paucity of incident. It does not divide the career of Jesus, as the other three do, into a period in Galilee in northern Palestine, a journey to Jerusalem, and one single, fateful visit to Jerusalem. Instead, Jesus moves rather freely from Galilee to Jerusalem and back, and hence he has been in Jerusalem several times before the last events. In John, the trial and death of Jesus take place on the day before the Passover; in the other three, the events take place on the first day of Passover.

Two of the Gospels, Mark and John, do not describe the birth of Jesus, or his boyhood. They plunge us immediately into his career at his maturity. Matthew and Luke relate, in differing ways, the miraculous birth of Jesus; Matthew passes immediately to the mature Jesus of Mark, while Luke offers one single boyhood incident—at twelve Jesus was taken by his parents to Jerusalem to the Temple—and then proceeds to material which is found in Mark (though Luke alters the sequence of the material).

Matthew, Mark, and Luke describe briefly the career of Jesus in Galilee, in northern Palestine (Matthew 3–18; Mark 1–9; Luke 3:1–9:50). All three then relate that Jesus journeyed from Galilee to Jerusalem. According to Matthew and Mark, the route which Jesus took led him eastward across the Jordan, then southward; he recrossed the Jordan at Jericho and went northwestward from Jericho to Jerusalem. According to Luke (9:51–18:14), the route which Jesus took led him due south, without the two crossings of the Jordan. Jesus thereby traverses the territory of the Samaritans.[3]

Matthew, Mark, and Luke then describe the events in Jerusalem in the last week of Jesus' life, culminating in his arrest, trial, and crucifixion. Matthew describes the appearance of the resurrected Jesus in Galilee; Luke describes it as occurring in Emmaus, near Jerusalem; Mark does not contain an account of a resurrection appearance.[4]

Mark differs from Matthew and Luke in that he deals mostly with what Jesus did; Matthew and Luke contain in addition materials reporting what Jesus taught.

In John soliloquy is so much the main content that incident is very much less than that of Mark. Whereas Matthew, Mark, and Luke seem to describe Jesus as visiting Jerusalem only once, and that for the fateful visit, John, as we have said, seems to be reporting three or even four visits. Hence, John lacks a clear Galilean period, and he lacks the journey to Jerusalem; he comes into fuller accord, though, when once he depicts Jesus' final days in Jerusalem.

So relatively little material do the Gospels contain that even if there were no problem about contradiction, discordancies, and historical credibility, there would still be insufficient material for a biography, especially in the modern sense. We do not know for sure in what year Jesus was born. Matthew ascribes his birth to the reign of King Herod, who died in 4 B.C. It is conventional to attribute the birth of Jesus to Herod's last year. Because a certain historian of the sixth century, Dionysius Exiguus, erred when he equated Roman and Church history, we have inherited the anomaly that Jesus was born in 4 B.C. As to the year of the death of Jesus, the data that we have inform us that he was thirty (Luke 3:23) or less than fifty[5] (John 8:57). The term which Pontius Pilate served as the Roman governor encompassed A.D. 26–36; the death of Jesus took place in that span of time, but in just what year we do not know.

We know only vaguely the environment and the times. Palestine had become a Roman province in 63 B.C., ending the independence of the Hasmonean dynasty which had begun in 150 B.C. Though the government was Roman, not Grecian, the Romans in the eastern part of the Empire had succumbed to Grecian culture, with the result that Grecian civilization was well represented in Palestine. Herod, in 37 B.C., took from the Hasmoneans the limited self-rule which the Romans allowed and became the king with Roman consent. Herod was as intent on being Grecian as on being a Jew, so that under him Greek influences (theaters, temples, schools) increased. After his death in 4 B.C., the Romans divided his territory into three parts: the kingdom of Judea under his son Archelaus; Galilee under Herod Antipas; and Trachonitis and other territories under Philip, a third son.

The Romans deposed Archelaus in A.D. 6 and banished him to Gaul, that is, to France. "Procurators" ruled Judea from A.D. 6 to A.D. 38, after which time, Herod Agrippa, Herod's grandson, received the limited throne. In Jesus' lifetime, oppression by Roman soldiers, and Jewish resistance to it, was an ordinary experience. In such oppression, Jews turned to their sacred literature for comfort and encouragement.

In this literature they read the assurance given through such prophets as Ezekiel that oppression was not destined to be eternal, nor misfortune unending. Through God's help the evil times would turn to good. Again, so went the comforting message, some descendant of David would occupy the throne of Judea. In Roman times, one who exalted a descendant of David could be decrying the later Hasmoneans who were wretches, and the Herodians who were worse. In Palestine, the symbol of making a man king was not to crown him, but to anoint him with oil. The Hebrew word for "anointed" is *Mashiah;* the word is usually spelled in English Messiah.

Adversity intensified Jewish yearning for the Messiah, and intensified yearning embroidered the achievement expected of him when in due time he would arise. Certainly he would destroy the foreigners occupying the country; since Jews were at that time already spread throughout the civilized world, the Messiah would miraculously gather the dispersed back to Palestine to the reconstituted proper kingdom.

The thought of the time gives us not a single set of Messianic hopes but a series of related expectations, overlapping and yet slightly differing from each other. In some thought, the achievements of the Messiah would be such as to usher in the awaited "last judgment," when God would redress the wrongs of the past. Some thought held that all men would be resurrected and then stand judgment; other thought held that all men would stand trial and only those declared innocent would be resurrected. The embroidery of Messianic thought extended its content beyond what was found in the Jewish sacred literature. Much of it, indeed, was less literally Scripture than it was a product of meditation on what was in the Hebrew Bible. Thus, the association of the Messiah and resurrection is post-biblical, and not biblical. Indeed, Jews did not agree with each other on many questions in which biblical views were extended into post-biblical times. Resurrection provided one of the disputes between the Pharisees and the Sadducees.

It is normal in the scholarly literature to take a cue from Josephus and to suppose that Jews in the days of Jesus fell into four camps, Pharisees, Sadducees, Essenes, and the Fourth Philosophy. This last group got its quaint name because Josephus described the first three as philosophies, and, lacking a name for the last, he gave it a number. Since Josephus was writing for Greek readers, and indulging in propaganda, we should take with many grains of salt his depiction of these groups as philosophies; we should be amusedly skeptical at his description of the Pharisees as Stoics, and the Essenes as Pythagoreans.[6] We would do well to understand the Fourth Philosophy as patriotic guerrillas rather than thinkers. We should not assume that four groups exhausted the groupings, nor should we delude ourselves into thinking that we know more about them than we do. Of these four, only two, Pharisees and Sadducees, are mentioned in the New Testament.

There the Sadducees are depicted as having with Jesus a dispute comparable to what is confirmed by rabbinic literature and by Josephus, namely, that the Pharisees asserted that resurrection[7] was a true and valid belief and, just as importantly, that it is found in the Five Books of Moses. The Sadducees denied both the belief in resurrection and also that it is found in the Five Books. (Resurrection is explicit only in Daniel of all the thirty-nine books; it is likely that in Jesus' time Daniel was as yet not uniformly regarded as part of Scripture.) The Pharisees could not point to a clear and unmistakable passage; the most they could do was to find a passage to which they had an interpretation congenial to them; the Sadducees denied both the aptness of the specific interpretation and, indeed, the general proposition that Scripture could be interpreted away from its literal sense.

The Pharisees espoused the principle that Scripture could be interpreted unliterally, and they also held that they were in possession of a body of interpretive conclusions which was a legacy from the age of Moses. It may possibly clarify the issue to use in changed form an ancient example. Scripture declares "You shall not burn a fire in all your dwellings on the Sabbath." The Pharisees declared that the emphasis is on *you;* Jews may not burn a fire but may hire a Gentile to do it for them; or, if one interprets burn in the sense of kindle, then the kindling could be forbidden, but a large and slow fire lit on Friday could properly provide warmth throughout the Sabbath. The issue between the Sadducees and the Pharisees was whether the wording of Scripture or the intent was decisive. The Pharisees were prepared not only to interpret Scripture so as to penetrate beyond unviable literalism into viable intent, but they believed that their deductive interpretations were validly revealed to Moses and transmitted from his time orally. The New Testament calls this body of oral interpretations "the tradition of the elders"; Jews call it the "oral Torah." [8]

We have inherited no literature at all from the Sadducees; we know of them only from their opponents, and only with respect to a limited array of doctrines. Pharisaic literature is abundant, but it dates in its written forms pre-eminently from a period much later, so that we have little secure data about Pharisaism in the period of Jesus. As to the Essenes, the Jewish preacher-philosopher Philo of Alexandria (20 B.C.–A.D. 40) gave a portrait of them which raises the double problem of how much he knew at first hand and how much his strange theosophy might have led him to attribute to them qualities which they may or may not have possessed. A Roman, Pliny, wrote a short paragraph about them in A.D. 67; Josephus, writing between A.D. 90 and 95, gives more data, but it conflicts with much of Philo's and it is also propagandistic. When we deal with the Essenes, we deal with uncertain, unreliable data; and even if it were certain and reliable, we should still be in the dark about the connection in religious atmosphere and influence between Galilee in the north and the Essenes who presumably were in the south. The over-praised Dead Sea scrolls, especially the "sectarian" documents, a small portion of the scrolls, at best throw light on the Judaisms of the time, but not specifically on Jesus. The Essenes go unmentioned in both New Testament and rabbinic literature. As to the "Fourth Philosophy," we may possibly best understand it as a sporadic, unorganized, recurrent impulse of activists, and leave it at that.

In sum, we know the immediate age of Jesus only in broad outline. We do not know, for example, if the title "rabbi" was already in common use in his day, or if it waited two or more decades. We do not know if that unique development, the synagogue, was in Jesus' day the act of meeting, or, as it was later, the place of meeting and hence an edifice. Josephus gave us information about the Temple, and the hereditary priesthood which conducted it, and that information, plus the Bible, plus rabbinic literature, combine to provide a reasonably clear picture of the sacrificial cult. We can see in some clarity that the Temple was priestly and the synagogue lay; we can see that animal sacrifice was central in the Temple, while Scripture was central in the synagogue, and that animal sacrifice was never part of the synagogue practice. We can conjecture that the scribe was the scriptural expert and teacher whose role passed to the rabbi. The "assembly" or "council," which Jews called Sanhedrin, by Semitizing the Greek word *synhedrion*, had certain prerogatives relating to the governing of Jews, but the exact rights which it had under either a Jewish ruler or under a Roman governor are also uncertain. We find also some surprising and dubious materials about priests—"chief priests" is a New Testament term unknown, and quite unlikely, in other Jewish literature. But for all that we do know, there is more that we do not know.

We do not know to what extent other compositions written in that age circulated and to what extent they were influential. Some such writings never achieved a place in the Bible, and, uncopied, they largely perished; some were translated into Greek and were preserved by Christianity. Among the writings which failed to gain a full and acknowledged status were some which are termed apocalyptic. The word apocalypse means "revelation"; the writings claimed to convey God's revelations of those events which were to happen at the end of time; and to the extent that Messianic thought in part dealt with the end of time, there is some connection between apocalyptic writing and messianism, but the precise connection is far from clear to us.

An ordinary practice followed by scholars is to search for confirming (or denying) data in relation to an ancient writer under study. In no area has this practice been followed as assiduously as in the case of the Gospel materials. What we find, if we may summarize it over simply, is the phenomenon of a general concord between the Gospels and what we reconstruct, despite missing pieces, of the Judaism of the time. In an abundance of areas we find ourselves confronted with detached problems, but a general concord does exist.

The uncertainties about the Jewish scene in the age of Jesus are kindred to the central problem of Jesus himself. The four Gospels, as we have seen, turn out to furnish contradictory information. Not only as one moves from Gospel to Gospel, but within one single Gospel, contradictions exist. These problems have raised for modern scholars the tremendous issue of how historically reliable the Gospels are.

The issue of historical reliability exists on a number of levels. To the modern skeptic who does not believe in miracles, historical reliability is an issue in the account of Jesus' walking on the water, his cures and exorcisms, his resurrection, and his ascension into heaven. On a different level is the issue of whether Jesus went to Jerusalem on the route described by Mark, or the route described by Luke, for the two routes mutually exclude each other. Did he completely forbid divorce, as Mark 10:1–12 has it, or did he allow it for adultery, as Matthew 19:1–12 relates? Did the events of his last week bring to the mind of Gospel writers passages from Psalms (especially 22 and 69), or did the Gospel writers draw from Psalms 22 and 69 the inspiration to invent for the life of Jesus those details which the Psalms contain? Did Jesus enter Jerusalem riding on one animal, as Mark tells, or two as Matthew relates; or is the entry narrative a fiction suggested by Zechariah 9:9? Did Jesus drive the money-changers from the Temple, or did a pious writer draw the motif from the last verse of Zechariah, and attribute it to Jesus?

Many Christians hold the Gospels to be divinely written, and hence free from error and contradiction. Other Christians attribute a divine status to them, yet stress the human factor involved in their composition. From roughly 1800 to our day, scholars, including loyal Christians, have studied the Gospels in much or exactly the same way as other ancient writings are studied. The prerequisite to any assessment of Jesus is an informed assessment of the Gospels.

It comes as a surprise to Christians as well as to Jews that by common scholarly agreement the Gospels are not the earliest

Christian writings, though they deal with the earliest events. Paul's Epistles are the oldest Christian writings.

Strangely, Paul gave little data about Jesus. We know from him only that Jesus was crucified, that Paul believed he was resurrected, that Jesus had a brother named James, and that Jesus taught that divorce was prohibited.

Whatever may be the reason for the absence of information about Jesus, this much is clear, Paul was interested in the significance of Jesus and not in details about him. One might say that Paul tried to tell us what Jesus was, not who he was. To Paul, Jesus was a human being who represented an interval in the eternal career of a divine being.[9]

Paul was not the only person who inferred from the tradition he had learned that Jesus had been vouchsafed a special resurrection and that Jesus was more than a man. Other minds too held comparable opinions. In the Gospels, which were written after Paul's time, Jesus is not a man. The Gospels in telling about Jesus are dealing also with the human career of a being considered divine. The Gospels were composed out of that same atmosphere of faith in the supernatural character of Jesus. As a consequence, aspects of the thought of the age of Paul and his fellow interpreters, concerning *what* Jesus was, merged with the body of older traditions, concerning *who* Jesus was, to swell the quantity of the total tradition out of which the Gospels were written.

These traditions about Jesus did not circulate unchanged; rather, they grew, they altered, they deepened in recognizable and often purposeful ways. We can see this especially in the accounts of the last week of Jesus' life, if we will note the changing part of Pilate from the small role he plays in Mark to the more elaborate (and more innocent) role he plays in Matthew and in Luke. We can see it in Mark's silence about Jesus' birth and compare it with Matthew's account in which Jesus, like Moses, almost died in the slaughter of innocent babes decreed by a wicked king, and in Matthew's having Jesus' father take him to Egypt (where Moses had been) so that Jesus could be summoned out of Egypt.

There was, then, a body of traditions about Jesus, and to this body the growing group of followers, soon to be termed "the Church," added both matters of theology and products of its meditative piety. As a consequence, the Gospels provide the student with a mixture of materials which reliably reflect Jesus but also reflect the opinions of the developing Church.

If we assume that the Gospels contain both reliable materials and also accretions, additions from later times, then the next question can be this: is it possible through objective study, through painstaking, fair-minded analysis, to separate these two from each other? Is it possible to separate the Jesus of reliable history from the Jesus of legend and the Jesus of theological belief? Is it possible to separate the man, purely the man, Jesus, from the view of him as divine? [10]

The wish to separate the human Jesus from the divine may or may not be legitimate, but one must be warned that such a separation goes against the grain of historic Christianity's writings. In those Jesus was held to be both fully human and fully divine. There were occasional voices in the early Church which, certain of his divinity, expressed various reservations about his full humanity. By and large such voices were deemed to be wrong, to be heretical, for ancient Christianity insisted as fully on the humanity of Jesus as on his divinity. In the past two hundred years, especially among Protestants and even more especially among radical or secular interpreters, the situation has become reversed, for the expressed reservations have been about his divinity, with his full humanity emerging as certain.

There is by now a history of scholarship at least two centuries old which dedicated itself to separating the human from the divine Jesus. I shall adopt some of the terminology of that scholarship in that I shall speak of Jesus, meaning thereby the man, and of the Christ, meaning thereby the divine.

Notes

1. There are a few direct mentions of Jesus in the Talmud, and a few passages about one Balaam which some have interpreted to be a cryptic, and hence indirect, mention. This Talmudic material, which is much later than the age of Jesus, has been studied and restudied with one principal objective, to determine whether these passages are or are not based on New Testament materials. If they are, then the conclusion is that the Talmud does furnish independent evidence about Jesus; if they are not, then the Talmud does not furnish such evidence. The view of most Talmudic scholars, for example, Jacob Z. Lauterbach, "Jesus in the Talmud," in *Rabbinic Essays*, pp. 473ff., is that the passages all reflect Christian tradition, not an independent Jewish tradition. Goldstein, *Jesus in the Jewish Tradition*, has a contrary view. My opinion is that Lauterbach is right. But even if one follows Goldstein, what he ends up with is so little material as to make it useless, except for one purpose. It can serve as one more tool to refute those who deny there ever was a Jesus. I do not think this particular tool is needed.

2. The duplicated material in Matthew and Luke is conventionally referred to by the letter Q. It stands for the German word *Quelle*, "source," and it reflects the theory that Matthew and Luke borrowed the non-Marcan overlapping material from a hypothetical source no longer extant. See below, p. 77.

3. These people were, from the standpoint of Jews, only quasi-Jews; they worshipped the Jewish God and held sacred the first six of the thirty-nine books of the Hebrew Scriptures; they were descended from importees into the northern areas after 721 B.C., when the Assyrians had transplanted the northern ten tribes to some eastern land. The importees, as we read in II Kings 17, blended their transported paganism with Jewish worship. Jews considered them improper as people and improper in their worship; the Samaritans had similar kindly thoughts about Jews. About 200 Samaritans survive today.

4. Two different endings make good the deficiency, but these endings are found in only a handful of manuscripts of Mark.

5. Some texts of John 8:57 read forty, not fifty.

6. *Antiquities* XV, X, 4; *Vita* II.

7. Resurrection and immortality have it in common that they deal with the fate of man, but they are quite different. Resurrection concedes that death takes place, but implies that life is subsequently restored. Immortality denies that death takes place. Most Jews and Christians of our day give lip service to resurrection by misinterpreting it as though it means immortality of the *soul*. Resurrection, of course, applies to the body.

8. The artificiality of the Pharisaic methods is, or should be, patent. It is, however, universal in religious bodies which have a sacred Scripture that they

need to develop a body of clarifying interpretation, or else become trapped in the *cul de sac* of literalism. Christianity and Islam have their "traditions of the elders." The Catholics and the Protestants have developed somewhat divergent "traditions," for the Protestants denied the accumulated body of Catholic tradition, went back to Scripture—and promptly revived "traditions."

9. See below, pp. 41–3.

10. A genuine understanding of this question is meaningless without some basic knowledge. For a Jew who has little or no acquaintance with the contents of the Gospels, a careful reading, indeed a study, is recommended.

CHAPTER 3 · The Divine Christ

There can be a profound difference in two intimately related questions. To ask, "Who was Jesus?" is to inquire into questions of a person and his career, in time and place. To ask "What was Jesus?" is to inquire into the views and opinions and conceptions about that person. While Judaism and Christianity came to a parting of the ways on several issues, the principal issue was this second question. In early Christianity, those Jews who believed that Jesus was the Messiah formed the nucleus from which the new religion emerged, while those Jews who did not believe him to be the Messiah remained outside the group.

The "Messiah" did not remain one single idea within the new group; rather, it grew both by adding some facets to the usual Jewish view and also by the dropping of Jewish facets, and one can speak, along the lines of Protestant and secular thought, of the development of the Messianic idea, or, in terms of Catholic thought, of the unfolding of man's grasp of the Messianic idea. The difference here is that the Catholics would seem to maintain that the idea was eternal and immune from development, and it was only man's understanding which developed, while Protestants would seem to hold that the idea itself developed. In either case, the Messiah at one stage represented a complex of ideas and opinions not wholly identical with the opinions of later days and later places. What is consistent is that Jews by and large abstained from sharing the Christian estimate of what Jesus was at all such stages.

We can speak of the usual view of the Messiah, and list here its usual component elements. To repeat what we have touched on already, the Jewish Messianic expectations were not single or monolithic, and there were some slight variations in details, yet a certain pattern is tolerably discernible. Consistently the Messianic thought and expectation flourished in the ages in which the Jewish people, or the Jewish nation, was in some dire strait, a situation brought about usually by the power of some foreign nation. This domination by wicked men would be ended, so it was believed, through the intervention of God. Specifically, some day there would arise an agent of God by whom or through whom the dire and dismal situation would be completely reversed. Jews had had a king from the time of Saul in the eleventh pre-Christian century until the Babylonian exile in the sixth; the early Messianic thought in the period of the Babylonian exile consisted primarily of the double hope that Jews would return to Palestine from Babylonia and that there the dynasty of David would return to the throne. As to the connection of the Messiah and the throne, the act by which a man was made king, which elsewhere was that of putting a crown on his head, was, among Jews, that of anointing him with oil. Hence, "the anointed one" was the king de jure, even though obstacles might linger on to impede him from being king de facto. The Hebrew for "the anointed one" is Messiah, and Messiah translated into Greek is Christos, which in English is shortened into Christ. Nothing in the mere word Christ relates it to Jesus; the association of Jesus and Christ is historical, not linguistic.

In the age of Jesus, as we have said, Palestine was a Roman possession, with its Jewish rulers subject to Rome. Hence, the

Messiah in the days of Jesus was expected to destroy the power particularly of Rome, to inaugurate a dynasty of the proper line, that of David, in place of the improper Hasmoneans, who had usurped the throne, and the even more improper Herodians. Also, since Jews were scattered throughout the then known world, the Messiah was expected to spur and enable the exiles to return to Palestine.

Moreover—and here an opinion reflecting specifically the age of Jesus entered in—events of so great a magnitude would seem to be such as to usher in the long-awaited final judgment of God; and since in a sizable portion of the population there existed a belief in resurrection, the latter became intertwined with both Messianic thought and with the expectation that the final judgment might be imminent. The formulations of Messianic thought did not always entirely accord, for in one pattern it was believed that the resurrection of all who had ever lived would occur and then the final judgment take place; another pattern held that the final judgment would take place and those who passed muster would be resurrected. In either case, the advent of the Messiah would usher in the final judgment and the new age.

The Messianic expectations, then, were a blend of both the divine and human facets, for, while God's part in the events was expected, the Messiah himself could have been only human, though sent by God. This human activity could seem to the Romans to be strictly a man-made affair and classifiable with insurrection. The Romans could be expected to be as antagonistic to a Messianic claimant in the same measure that Jews could exult in his appearance.

Jesus was neither the first nor the last in the long history of Judaism by whom or for whom the claim was made that he was the long-awaited Jewish Messiah.[1] It would have been normal for such a person deemed the Messiah to attract followers and partisans, and for there to be on the sidelines those who waited to see whether the outcome of events fulfilled the expectations and specifications or not, before deciding whether the particular person was or was not the Messiah. For a claimant to be hailed initially in no way meant that he continued to elicit acceptance; and every Messianic claimant in Judaism has begun with, or quickly gained, broad acceptance and ended in general rejection. In the case of Jesus, as we have said, his partisans held after his death that he had been vouchsafed a special resurrection, and out of this belief proceeded a new and differing interpretation of the role of the Messiah. But among those who were not his partisans and followers, the opinion was that since those things specifically expected to come about from or through the Messiah had not eventuated, then Jesus could not be, and was not, the long-awaited Messiah. In a word, the people who did not accept Jesus as the Messiah rejected the claims because the expectations did not materialize. The power of Rome was not broken, the Davidic line was not restored, the scattered were not miraculously restored to Palestine; day-to-day life went on as before.

In its true context, at this stage, the issue was strictly an internal Jewish one, involving Jews who accepted the Jew Jesus as the Jewish Messiah and Jews who did not. Only much later, when the Gentiles supplanted the Jews in the new movement, could the question be posed in the form, why did *the* Jews not accept Jesus as the Messiah; in this latter time the definition of the Messiah had become notably transformed from something involving specific and temporal characteristics into something involving more suprahuman abstractions.

Those Jews who had accepted Jesus as the Messiah, despite his death on the cross, made an initial significant alteration in the Messianic pattern, changing it, as it were, from one single event, ushering in the great climax, into two parts, preparation first, and after an interval, the climax. This alteration became conformed to the reality that Jesus had died on the cross; but, so it was firmly believed, he had been quickly resurrected and then had ascended to heaven, there to await the appropriate time for his second coming. It was the latter that was viewed as the climax; his initial coming had been the preparation. That "second coming" is still awaited in Christendom and is a basic tenet in orthodox Christian conviction, though in established and sedate churches it does not loom centrally or vividly.

The developed conviction that the Messiah's program consisted of the past preparatory step and of the future expectation naturally prompted speculation into the nature of Jesus. That he had been vouchsafed a special resurrection and has ascended to heaven to await the time of his return could, and patently would, imply that he was in some special way more than human, and hence in some special way divine. The literature of the New Testament unhappily does not give us a quick and simple summary of the manner in which the views unfolded that Jesus was more than human. I shall here essay such a summary, but I own that it is based on uncertain inferences, and is not fully susceptible of documentary substantiation. This is especially the case in the first steps, in which I would summarize, in the phrase "Son of Man," the view held that Jesus was more than human.

It is probable that no biblical phrase has attracted more theories than this phrase "Son of Man." The expression is used in many passages in Ezekiel where, admittedly on all sides, it means no more than "man." Ezekiel flourished in the sixth pre-Christian century. The phrase as it is more directly related to New Testament thought occurs in Daniel 7:13. There we read of a vision of what is to occur at the final judgment, and in that vision the heathen nations are represented by horrendous beasts, while Israel is represented, in contrast, by "one like unto a *son of man.*" If we are justified in binding this passage in Daniel with Messianic expectations, as indeed we are, then it becomes intelligible that the expression "Son of Man" could become synonymous for the Messiah. In many passages in the Gospels (with their relatively scant use of the word Messiah) Jesus is equated with the "Son of Man," and in a great many of the passages he is portrayed in direct quotations as using the expression with reference to himself. A good many modern scholars hold to the opinion that these passages represent words attributed to Jesus by the developing Church, rather than authentic words of Jesus, but that is an academic, antiquarian question for which we need not indulge in a digression. This much is alone relevant, that Jesus was viewed in his lifetime, or shortly thereafter came to be viewed, as this supernatural "Son of Man," whose abode, in the vivid imagery of Daniel, was in heaven, and who was destined to "come on the clouds"; in the Gospels Jesus is conceived as having returned to heaven after the resurrection, some day to *return* on the clouds.

That Jesus was viewed as the "supernatural" Son of Man falls short of specifying the exact nature of his supernatural being; it was an assertion, not a dictionary definition. Moreover, it was an assertion that was expressed fully within the framework of segments of Judaism, and was in no way, in itself, a product of Gentile thinking. We may summarize this aspect of our discussion in this way: once the followers of Jesus were convinced that he was resurrected, there was nothing inconsistent with their Judaism in conceiving of him as the heavenly Son of Man. On the other hand, those who did not believe that he was resurrected denied that he was the Son of Man, not so much because they disbelieved in the *idea*, but because they did not believe in this particular identification.

The movement of the resurrected Jesus spread outside Palestine, and, of course, into the Graeco-Roman world. In that altered environment there took place another shift in the manner of describing the supernatural nature of Jesus. On the one hand, the shift involved the winnowing out of aspects of Jewish Messianic thought. Such matters as the destruction of the Roman colonial power over Palestine and the restoration of a Jewish dynasty, with Jews reassembled from all over the world, scarcely had the same significance for Gentiles in Athens or in Rome as it had for Jews in Galilee. Indeed, among Gentiles in the Grecian areas the significance of the supernatural Jesus lay in his meaning to the whole world, rather than in his meaning for strictly Jewish history. The New Testament documents preserve what are only vague hints, or dim vestiges, of the specific Jewish Messianic hopes. A passage, Acts 1:6, portrays the disciples, after Jesus' resurrection, asking Jesus, "Will you at this time restore the kingdom to Israel?" [2] Additional vague clues, or remainders of Jewish thought, are the allusion to Jesus at the trial and crucifixion as the "King of the Jews" [3] (Mark 15:2, 12, 18, 26, and 32; Matthew 27:11, 29, 37, and 42; Luke [4] 23:2–3 and 38; John 18:33, 39; 19:3, 14–15, 19–21). Perhaps there is some relevancy to this discussion in the passage,

John 18:36, in which Jesus is portrayed as replying to Pilate, "My kingship is not of this world . . ."; perhaps this passage clearly repudiates whatever lingering connection there was between the messiahship and Jewish national aspirations. There are some who interpret Luke 13:1, which mentions "Galileans whose blood Pilate had mingled with their sacrifices," as an allusion to the kind of patriotic, anti-Roman activity which may possibly also have accompanied the movement led by Jesus (see below, p. 53).

We have, then, at best in the New Testament only the dimmest associations of Jesus' messiahship with Jewish national hopes. Perhaps one goes beyond the evidence even in supposing that these were winnowed out of the developing Christian conceptions, for to speak of their being winnowed out implies that they were once present, but confirming evidence cannot adequately bear out that they were.

Yet still another facet must here be noticed. Anointment to Jews was a rite; to Greeks it was a form of cosmetics. To Greeks, the expression "Jesus the anointed" was either meaningless or vapid; as a consequence, the phrase Jesus *the* Christ became changed into Jesus Christ, or Christ Jesus, as if "Christ" were a name, a title, and not a rendering of "anointed." Perhaps the effect of the change could be made more vivid by our noticing the difference in sound and effect between the title James the Prince and the name James Prince. The title, as it were, came close to being submerged into merely a name. I have here oversimplified, and shall proceed to modify the oversimplification; let it suffice for our purposes that in the world of Greek Christians the word Christ had connotations which on the one hand lacked what the Hebrew *mashiah* necessarily implied, and on the other hand gained associations quite lacking from the Hebrew approach. To Greek Christians the term Christ had the clear implication of a divine being.

The New Testament presents a variety of titles or terms which reflect the belief in the divine nature of Jesus. One of these is Son of God. To Jews this term, if used figuratively, would have raised no objection, for it is a frequent phrase in the Tanak; Deuteronomy 14:1 reads, "You are the sons of the Lord your God." If used literally or quasi-literally, Jews would have objected, and especially so to limiting sonship to Jesus. In the New Testament, the phrase is in some respects a little indistinct, but what is clear about it is its use to allude to the divine nature attributed to Jesus.

Still another term, "Lord," occasions difficulties in comprehension on the part of Jews. We Jews use the word "Lord" as an exact synonym for God. In the Greek world, however, the term had a number of additional overtones and usages. "Lord" is the English translation of the Greek word *kyrios*. In Greek *kyrios* had the basic meaning of owner, possessor, master. In speaking of a person (in direct address the form changes to *kyrie*) the word meant something like "sir." Again, among the Greeks, who possessed a whole pantheon of gods, *kyrios* was used as the title for the particular deity who was the patron of some religious cult or association, for example, the Lord Sarapis, or the Lord Hermes. In such a usage, *kyrios* did not imply sole deity, but rather of the many deities that particular one to whom the cult was dedicated. In the New Testament usage, the title *kyrios* as applied to Jesus (except for those passages in which it means simply "sir") equates him with divinity, but does not equate him with God. The Epistles of Paul frequently use the expression "the Lord Jesus," in the sense of a divine being, but not in the sense of God Himself. This is illustrated in the passage, I Corinthians 8:5–6, which tells that for Christians there is but "one God, the Father, and one Lord, Jesus Christ." Perhaps we may set beside this quotation another passage, Acts 2:36, in which we read that God had made Jesus "both Lord and Christ. . . ."

How much of the attribution of divinity to Jesus took place within Palestinian Christianity is uncertain. Unquestionably such a belief arose among those of his followers who believed that he had been resurrected, for the special, miraculous resurrection could imply that Jesus was more than a man, and therefore in some sense divine. Some scholars believe that the title "Lord," in Aramaic *mar*,[5] arose in Palestine; most, however, attribute the title to Gentile Christianity outside Palestine.

If we press on to ask the question, what was the nature of the

divinity of Jesus, a divinity which in early Christianity fell short
of identifying him as God, then in addition to Lord another term,
"*Logos*," merits attention here. The divine Jesus is explicitly identified with *Logos*, as we shall see, but briefly and laconically. The
term *Logos* was an ancient Greek one, and was given currency in
the age of Jesus among Greek Jews, especially in the writings of
Philo of Alexandria, 20 B.C.–A.D. 40. To see how Greek Jews
treated *Logos* can help us, if we are cautious, in understanding
what Christians had in mind when they identified Jesus in that
way. Cautious, for there are differences as well as similarities between the Jewish and Christian *Logos*.

If the question is asked, what was meant by *Logos*, then in the
interest of clarity we might first ask, what is the religious or
philosophical question to which the term *Logos* is the answer?
We might say that *Logos* is the endeavor to solve a recurring
problem in religious thought, the attempt to reconcile the question of the remote yet immanent God. Man in his thoughtful, pious
moments tends, as it were, so to aggrandize God that the result
could be a conception of God far removed from and over and
above and even outside this world. Yet, on the other hand, there
is a sense in which a remote God is meaningless to man, and the
concept of God is applicable to man's life only insofar as he is
near at hand, and in this world, available to man to assist him, or
for man to pray to. How, then, can man conceive of God as simultaneously "transcendent," above and even outside the world, and
yet "immanent," within the world and available to man? Late
Palestinian Jewish thought "solved" this dilemma by envisaging
angels who were the bridge between man and the remote God.
That thought which conceived of angels was often intuitive, folk-
loristic, even "mythic." Graeco-Jewish thought, on the other
hand, was rationalistic, "dialectical" (that is, strictly logical), and
disinclined to the mythic, even when it accepted the data of
myths. *Logos*, which was deeply imbedded in Graeco-Jewish
thought, was the device whereby Greek Jews solved the dilemma
of a God who was both transcendent and immanent.

What, then, was *Logos*? The term can be, and has been, translated by differing English terms. It means something along the

lines of "logical thinking," and, at the same time, it connotes the content of that logical thought. We might summarize it in the word "reason," or summarize it, as Christians have, in the term "Word." We might render it by "intelligence," or "wisdom," or even by the double word, "world-soul." From its Greek background, the term has to do with wisdom, which is gained through correct logic, and which is available to such people as have the capacity to reason correctly and thereby to acquire, each person for himself, some individual portion or possession of the universal wisdom and knowledge. From its Jewish side, God's revelation was obviously wise; hence revelation, God's disclosure, and wisdom, man's achievement, were closely related. So closely were they deemed to be related that in late Palestinian Jewish thought revelation and wisdom had become virtually identified. When this Jewish identification of revelation and wisdom encountered the Greek world, the substance of Greek wisdom was also assimilated into it, with the result that the philosophy of Plato or of the Stoics could be encompassed within Jewish revelation-wisdom, to the extent that it seemed correct thinking. The ancient Greek term *Logos* became the principal term to express the idea that divine revelation and universal wisdom were one and the same thing and could serve as a bridge between God and man.

As to man and God, one might arrive at views of their relationship in two different ways. One might look at the long flow of events of human history and make conclusions about God as the planner and guide of these events; this was the way of the ancient Hebrew prophets. Or one might analyze the nature of the world, as if it were static and not connected with events, as Plato and Aristotle had done; this was the way of the Greek Jews. Or, to rephrase this, the Greek Jew entered into philosophy only after he had reached his religious conviction; he began with the belief that God existed and that God had guided the events of the past, and from this belief he proceeded into his "static" analysis. This latter was very complicated. It involved his notice of the nature of man, a creature with passions and senses, but also a creature able to reason. He would explain the functioning of senses and of reason, and speak about wisdom, and about universal wisdom.

He could describe this universal wisdom as the "mind of God" or as "divine reason." When such matters are descriptive they remain within philosophy. They become religion when the assertion is next made that man's reason can ascend toward God and experience and encounter God's reason. This encounter occurs within this world; God Himself is above and beyond this world. Elsewhere I have suggested the analogy of the remote power plant and the light bulb in a room in my house. God, like the power plant, is remote. He comes into my room in the form of the light bulb, and I am able to experience the light bulb. *Logos*, like the light bulb, was the way, the form, the manner in which God was manifest and experienced in this world. The *Logos* served Greek Jews as the bridge to the remote, transcendent God in a way comparable to that served by angels in the thought of Palestinian Jews.

We must now turn to a distinction which is somewhat difficult to make. I can draw a line on a piece of paper; let us agree that this is a real line, for it is visible, and a chemist could show us that the graphite is different from the paper. On the other hand, we speak of the border between two states as a "line," a divider which surveyors can locate which separates two territories from each other. Such a line is not real in the same way as a pencil stroke on a piece of paper, but real in a different way, and the purpose it serves is real. In a third option, we speak of the "line" that separates love from hate, and we mean thereby neither the pencil stroke nor the surveyor's convention. This third line is in one sense real, but as compared with the other two lines, it is a figure of speech, and only that. We often use such figures of speech in our communication with each other: the *ideal* marriage, *pure* morality, *abstract* beauty, and the like. All such ideas are real enough that we utilize the phrases, but if we should be pushed, we might feel constrained to regard them as constructions of the mind and not as sheer, utter realities. They are like the line which separates love from hate, not like the line we draw on a piece of paper or the boundary line.

Was *Logos* a sheer, utter reality to Greek Jews, like a line on a paper, or was it a mental construction, like abstract beauty? The scholars differ in interpreting the material, and justly so; some passages tend to confirm one view and some the other. This issue cannot be resolved. Yet a number of comments can be made. Greek Jews, at the minimum, often treat *Logos* as a mere abstraction; they avoid attributing to it any location in space and time; hence, they ordinarily approach it on a theoretical basis, as a philosophical construct.

This Graeco-Jewish *Logos* serves as a way station for our understanding of the transition from the Palestinian Jewish Messianic idea to the Christian. Christian thought, as it developed, went beyond the Son of Man and identified Jesus and the *Logos*. There was already developed, among Greek Jews, a body of *Logos* thought close at hand for Christians to proceed on to their identification. The clearest such identification is in the first sentences of the Fourth Gospel, which I shall presently quote. But first the statement needs to be made that in Paul's Epistles the word Christ seems kindred to a synonym for *Logos*.[6] Paul reported having personally *experienced* the Christ. Hence, if the identification is justified, the *Logos* in Christian thought was not a mere abstraction as it may have been to Philo, especially since the main lines of the Christian tradition held that Jesus lived in a particular time and a particular age. A Christian could and would speak of *Logos* as a matter of experience, and not at all a merely mental construction; and he would contend that the *Logos*-Jesus was known to have lived in Galilee and in Judea in a specific period of time, born in the last year of Herod, and put to death in the term in which Pontius Pilate was the Roman Procurator.

The Fourth Gospel makes a clear identification of *Logos* and Christ. It begins with these words: "In the beginning was the *Logos* and the *Logos* was with God and the *Logos* was divine." The frequent translation is, "The Word was *God*"; there are disputes as to the best rendering. The Gospel goes on to make assertions, two of which have relationship to our context. The first of these is that the *Logos*, antecedently a divine spirit, had become bodily, "incarnate," in Jesus. The second assertion is that the *Logos* had created this world; in the words of John 1:3, "All things were made through him, and without him was not anything made that was made."

Let us imagine a Greek Jew, steeped in the thought of someone
like Philo of Alexandria, encountering this second contention, but
in isolation from the first. Not only would such a loyal Jew not
have disagreed, but he would have given enthusiastic assent, for
in Philonic thought the *Logos* is the immanent, this-worldly
aspect of the transcendent God. In many a passage Philo spoke
of the *Logos* in ways kindred to the New Testament way of
speaking of the *Logos*-Christ. As to the first assertion, my opinion
is this, that a Greek Jew would not have denied the *possibility* of
the incarnation, but would have either agreed or disagreed on
whether the possible incarnation of the *Logos* as Jesus had actually taken place. Philo, for example, contended that the three
visitors of Abraham in Genesis 18:2 were divine beings incarnated as men.

What is germane is our need to understand that the religious
currents in the first and second Christian centuries were varied
and complex, and it is unjust to view them as simple and subject
to neat categories. The substance of the views of a Greek Jew in
all likelihood was little known or debated in more than overtones
or nuances among Palestinian Jews. Some traces of these dim
echoes are known from rabbinic literature, for passages there alert
us to some perhaps hazy awareness of opinions about a *Logos*
who did the creating of the world, but the matured bent of Palestinian Jews was to reject any formulation of deity which appeared
to compromise strict monotheism. The opinion of Philo on the
Logos would have been as distasteful to a Palestinian Jew as
would have been the opinion of a Greek Christian on the *Logos*-
Christ. Indeed, the emergence of the passage, Deuteronomy 6,
"Hear O Israel, the Lord our God the Lord is One" to its eminence
as the watchword of rabbinic Judaism is to be explained as a
formulation which gave scriptural sanction to resisting any compromise of God's unity. Within Christendom the unequal battle
was fought between those triumphant in their view on the Christ-
Logos as a reality and those who viewed it as no more than a
mental construction, and who denied the reality and hence the

historicity of the incarnation. In the welter of conflicting opinions and judgments, clarity emerges for us only toward the
middle of the second century. By that time Greek Judaism was virtually defunct, and only Palestinian rabbinic Judaism was destined to survive; by that time there had already developed a main
stream of Christian thought which makes it possible to contrast
views as either central on the one hand or as peripheral on the
other; or to use instead such terms as "orthodox" on the one hand
and "heretical" on the other.

To a second-century Palestinian Jew, then, possessing no affinity
with Greek thought, the *Logos* idea, even as a mental construction, was uncongenial, for it compromised the unity of God; and
the view that the *Logos* and Jesus were bound up in each other
seemed to go further and to blaspheme that unity.

Yet another stage of development took place in Christendom, in
the late New Testament period or shortly after it. It was a pro-
gression which removed the distinction between *Logos* and God,
and which went from regarding Jesus as the *Logos* of God into
regarding him as the very "Godness of God." Perhaps this can
be restated in this way, that for many Christians Jesus ceased to
be identified *merely* with the *Logos,* and he came to be conceived
of instead as God Himself.

This development brought great contentions and strife into
Christianity. The central opinion held that Jesus was both God
and man, but theological exposition produced discordant and
contradictory opinions of the relative divinity and relative humanity within Christendom. What all Christians by and large agreed
on was that Jesus was divine; what they fought about was just
how human he was. Did he have one nature, or two? Was Mary
the mother of Christ Jesus, or was she also to be spoken of as
"mother of God"?

A Palestinian Jew, should he have the chance to overhear some
of the inner Christian disputations in the third century, would not
have been able, even if he tried, to penetrate the abstruse theological debates. It is not alone that he would have rejected the
conflicting Christian contentions, but, also, the self-contained and

isolated character of rabbinic Judaism would have impeded him from even beginning to comprehend the self-contained and isolated character of Christian theology. Had such a Jew, for example, encountered the trinitarian formula of Matthew 28:19, "the Father, Son, and Holy Spirit," [7] he would have rejected it as inconsistent with monotheism. He would not only have been convinced, as many Jews are mistakenly convinced still today, that Christianity is not a monotheism, but also he would not have believed that the God of Christianity is conceived of by the Christians as the God of Israel. Indeed, the trinitarian formula merits the focus in our discussion that on the one hand it is inherently *incomprehensible* to Jews, and on the other hand it ascribes to Jesus a divinity which Jews are unwilling to ascribe to any *man*.

When we Jews have understood Christian explanations, and when we have not, we have consistently rejected the Christian claims about Jesus. We have not believed that Jesus was the Messiah; we have not been willing to call him Lord; we have not believed that the *Logos* became incarnate as Jesus; we have not believed that Jesus was, or is, the very Godness of God.

In this light, matters such as the virgin birth in Matthew and in Luke, and the healings and the miracles of the Gospels, and the Christian forms of biblical proof-texting [8] stand disclosed as mere details. Jews, except for those Greek Jews who took the dead-end road of Philo, have always been immutably unitarians, and unable to acquiesce to a view about any man which raises him above the level of man and in any way equates him with God.

Perhaps in our day it is possible to say these things without giving inadvertent offense. Perhaps Christians have some interest in a straightforward but amicable expression by Jews of where they stand. Perhaps the diversity of Christian beliefs in our days puts the Jewish expression into a context of comparable and even similar expressions by Christians or quasi-Christians. But the amicable expression of such a view is a matter of relatively recent origin; in the early Christian centuries these expressions were received with extreme hostility. We Jews have faced the problem that orthodox Christian thought has regarded us as deicides, and even today we are sometimes called Christ-killers. Our defense has scarcely endeared us to orthodox Christians, for we have said that it was the Romans, not the Jews who killed Jesus, but it has been clear that we have not regarded Jesus as divine, and we are saying in effect that we are not deicides because we did not kill Jesus and, besides, he was not the deity.

We cannot in any honesty dissemble about our opinions. We do not see Jesus in the way that Christians do, and we cannot pretend that we do. Those of us who belong to the liberal interpretation of Judaism do not acknowledge adherence to the traditional Jewish view of the Messiah; therefore it is all the more impossible for us to acquiesce in the Christian views related to or derived from the traditional views. (Yet it need not follow that the basic disagreement on this central theological matter precludes an honest understanding of the differences, or a recognition of large areas of common interests, common ideals, and common privileges of co-operation between Christians and us.)

It is not alone that the abstract conception of the Christ is alien to us Jews, but the Christian conception of the significance of the career of the Christ Jesus is equally alien. It is a Christian belief that the crucifixion was an atoning death which opened to mankind man's redemption from sin. On the one level, we Jews have conceived of sin, atonement, and salvation in ways quite different from the Christian conception, and not only do we Jews abstain from sharing in the Christian belief, but the truth is that most of us fail to understand even what Christians mean in their use of these terms common to both religions, as Christians often fail to understand us in our use of these terms.

We Jews understand by sin, by and large, an act or action; by and large Christians understand by it a state, a condition of man. We Jews understand by atonement man's need of self-search for the purpose of understanding and of acknowledging his sinful acts, his need to feel a genuine regret, a genuine sense of repentance at his having committed them, and his dedication to a life as free as possible from such acts. It is a Jewish belief that when man atones, God may, if He so determines, forgive. We might put it in this way, that in the Jewish view man is prone to sinful acts, but man can atone, and God forgives.

In the Christian view man is in his innate nature a sinner, and atonement implies a change in man's nature. Man cannot unaided work this transformation; in other words, man himself cannot atone. Instead, atonement must be wrought for man by the Christ. In this sense, the death of the Christ Jesus is regarded as the act of atonement whereby man can be redeemed from his sinfulness; this is the meaning of the phrase, so often incomprehensible to Jews, that "Christ died for our sins." The various figures of speech in Christian lore are often only synonyms for these conceptions; the phrase, strange to Jewish ears, that one must be "washed in the blood of the lamb," stems from the identification made in the New Testament of the Christ with the "lamb led to slaughter" of Isaiah 53:7, with the result that the "blood of the lamb" is a colorful way of stating the belief in the atoning death of Jesus.

In the elaboration of the Christian view of the atoning death of the Christ, there developed the view that this single act opened the way to salvation both to all men who lived before Jesus' time (and hence Jesus is conceived of as having descended into hell to preach to souls there) and to all men born after his time. To the question, "How can a man benefit from the atoning death?"— among the answers given was that baptism wiped out man's sins, or that "faith" in the Christ brought man into the sharing in that benefit. Since our subject is Jesus, and not the broader topic of Christian doctrine and theology, it is not possible here to enter into a broader exposition of these matters. It must suffice to say that we Jews, cognizant that all men will sin, nevertheless do not conceive of man as a sinner. Sin as a *condition of man* is as unintelligible to us as sin as *act* is intelligible; and atonement which a man makes periodically, either on the Day of Atonement, or, as Judaism provides, whenever a man is moved to make it, roots the act of atonement within the lifetime of each individual man, and we readily understand it. We do not readily understand an act of atonement external to the lifetime of each individual man.[9] We do not believe that man needs baptism to wash his sins away; we believe that man must make his own atonement, not have atonement wrought for him.

The issue here is not whether the Jewish way is better, or the Christian way better, but only that these two ways are so different as to be to most Jews and Christians incomprehensible to each other. Most of us Jews never penetrate to the point of understanding what Christians mean by the atoning death of the Christ. Most of us do not accept it because it is so foreign to our basic intuition; those of us who achieve a tolerably correct understanding of it do not accept it because it is foreign to our convictions.

It is, however, not alone these specific items that mark off the Jewish religious mentality from the Christian. In a more general sense, Jewish thought is inherently concrete and practical, and hence Judaism, despite its bondage to the divine, is essentially humanistic. The Jewish counterparts of Christian medieval theology are, of course, comparable intellectual exercises, but they are ancillary and not quintessential in Judaism, and it was primarily in the medieval period that these Jewish theological writings arose and flourished. By and large the Christian way has been to ask the question, what shall a man believe, holding that the belief could and would lead man to appropriate action; the Jewish way has been to ask, what shall a man do, holding that what man does illuminates the antecedent, and even tacit, faith. Jews have seldom tried to define faith, and when they did so, the definitions came from sporadic individuals expressing an individual judgment. The Christian way, exemplified in the past and the present, has been to convene a Council of authorized persons to vote on and determine proper belief. Never once did Jews convene an assembly of authorized persons to debate and decide on some article of faith; common consent to an ancient tradition, and not explicit doctrines and dogmas, has marked the Jewish way. In Jewish history there are illustrious names of men who codified the *halacha*, "what man should do," and hence we Jews pay homage to Joseph Karo who had little philosophic bent, and we admire Maimonides' "Code" just as much as we do his reconciliation of Judaism and Aristotelianism in *Guide for the Perplexed*.

Christians from time to time wonder at our ability to reject what they conceive of as the climactic boon of God, and they occasionally charge us, in our form of monotheism and our relative paucity of theological inquiry, with failing to grasp the full profundity and deep richness of its Christian form. Sometimes Christians seem to me to say this in an understandable resentment of Jewish allegations that Christianity either is not monotheistic (of course it is!), or that Jewish monotheism is "purer" than Christian (of course it is not!). But there is a special pleading involved in such judgments, and there is no objective way by which we can measure the relative merits of the one expression of the common monotheism against the other expression. Mood and disposition, and conditioning, account for the preferences and prepossessions.

We Jews do not accept the saving death of Jesus because of our special mood and disposition and our conditioning to the problems of living and to the problems of religion. We are Jews, not Christians, and hence we do not share in the Christian beliefs in the significance of "the Christ and Him crucified." To us Jesus is never more than a man, and deeply as some of us Jews are able to sympathize with the tragedy of his life and death, we do not see in it any special working of the divine.

Notes

1. A considerable literature exists on the question of whether Jesus proclaimed himself the Messiah or whether it was the disciples who made the claim. Moreover, there are scholars who, in attributing the claim to the disciples, believe that it was not during Jesus' lifetime but only after his resurrection that the assertion was made. The haziness in the records accounts in good measure for these differences of opinion, though possibly modern dispositions combine with the haziness to yield the differing conclusions. The interpreter is on uncertain ground in judging the evidence, and he either leaves the question open or else espouses his particular opinion on the basis of his judgment about where the limited evidence seems to him to point. My own opinion is that the association of Jesus with Messianic claims did not await his death, but occurred in his lifetime. It is my opinion also that if

Jesus did not actively announce himself as the Messiah, he at least acquiesced in the identification which others made.

Quite as complicated and quite as uncertain is the question of in what sense Jesus was conceived of, or conceived himself, as the Messiah. Not only was there some range in the Messianic view among Jews, but the unfolding Christian thought extended this range. Admitting these uncertainties, my opinion is this, that there are emphases in Jewish messianism not found in Christian messianism, and that Christian messianism is marked by themes which the Jewish never developed. I believe that Christian messianism grew out of and away from Jewish messianism; I see development and also deliberate alteration and rejection of themes in the transition. In the text I describe this transition schematically for the sake of clarity, but I am aware that the schematization is overconfident. Beyond the issue of whether or not development is as clearly discernible as my text makes it, the resulting contrast between Jewish and Christian Messianic themes is in its own right quite reliable, though not nearly as simple as I necessarily present it.

2. The reply is: "It is not for you to know times or seasons which the Father has fixed by his own authority."

3. Whereas Mark 15:12 speaks of "the King of the Jews," the parallel as found in Matthew 27:17 speaks of "Jesus who is the Christ."

4. There are no direct parallels in Luke for Mark 15:12 and 18; as to Mark 15:32, the parallel in Luke 23:35 lacks the phrase "King of Israel."

5. The Aramaic phrase, *maran atha,* usually aggregated into the one word *maranatha,* occurs in I Corinthians 16:22. It means, "Our Lord, come!"

6. Paul did not explicitly identify *Logos* and Christ. This identification has been made by some modern scholars and denied by other scholars. Frank Porter seems to have denied the identification in *The Mind of Christ in Paul* (pp. 172–200), but even in denying it to Paul he conceded the possibility of it. The issue, a highly technical one, revolves in part over disputes as to whether or not Paul was truly the author of The Epistle to the Colossians which the New Testament ascribes to him.

7. The pre-modern English translations speak of "Holy Ghost," for what *ghost* used to mean is today better conveyed by *spirit*. The trinitarian phrase in its early days, before its elaboration and embellishment, seems to me not too difficult to define and explain, though Christians often assert that it is a "mystery" beyond explanation. It was, to my mind, a response to the implicit question, how does God come into relation with man and man with God? In the formulation, the Father is, of course, God, the remote, transcendent God; the son is the *Logos*-Christ, conceived of as having occurred in time and in a place, and thus having acted in that interval of time in which the *Logos*-Christ was the incarnate man Jesus. The Holy Spirit has been the immanent

spirit of God after the *Logos*-Christ reascended to heaven to await the time of the return. This view will, of course, be disputed by other interpreters.

8. Christians, in both early and in recent times, have used Old Testament passages as proof of Christian claims. They borrowed the method from Jews. Proof-texting usually involves reading into an Old Testament passage a special meaning which is often not actually there. When Christians confront Jews with such passages, they usually do not notice that they give the passages special meanings. Often, Christians, especially Fundamentalists, inquire of Jews how they can fail to admit Christian contentions in the light of Old Testament passages, especially passages in the Book of Isaiah. The answer is that Jews do not see in such passages the same meanings, especially the predictions about Jesus, which Christians see there. To repeat, the *method* is an ancient Jewish one which Christians borrowed; the content, once the method was borrowed, was, of course, congenial to Christian claims. Such proof-texting is frequent in Paul's Epistles and especially in the Gospel according to Matthew.

9. Christianity, of course, conceives of Christ's atoning death as available to each man in his own lifetime. The difference pointed to is that the act of atonement in Christian thought took place once, long ago, and for all time.

CHAPTER 4 · Jesus the Man

I THE RESEARCH ON THE LIFE OF JESUS

The approach of a Jew to Jesus takes its point of departure from the historical question, who was he? The issue which this chapter raises is whether the "historical" Jesus can be separated from the Christ of faith or from the Jesus of Christian piety. Can we isolate the man Jesus so as to have some objective attitude toward him? Can we so sift the documents of the New Testament, composed in faith in the supernatural Christ, and discover or "recover" Jesus the man, Jesus the Jew? When, in the early nineteenth century, the objective of Protestant scholarship became centered on the Jesus of history, the depth and breadth of that scholarship made some Jews feel compelled to give serious attention to him, and, indeed, there arose in some of them a tendency which has properly been called the "Jewish reclamation" of Jesus. Subtly connected with this "Jesus of history" has been the emergence of what one might call "the Jesus of Western society." This Jesus is not quite the same as the Jesus of historical scholars, but rather an intuitive assumption on the part of Western man that there are certain high points in human intellectual and spiritual attainment which characterized Jesus, and hence that Jesus the man represents a kind of benevolent humanitarianism to mankind at large and he serves as an exemplar, a model for the aspirations of the individual. This Jesus of Western culture is held to have been a man of keen insight into the psychology of men, a kindly and benevolent person who unbrokenly manifested good will, and whose mission in life was to bring about universal peace and to provide guidance for men in either solving the acute social, economic, and political problems of the age, or at least of setting forth the standards by which the problems might be solved. This Jesus of Western culture is only remotely connected with the Christ of Christian faith, and even less directly connected with the historical Jesus. When the ghetto walls fell, this Jesus of Western man came more and more into the ken of Jews in the West.

The Protestant scholarship on Jesus the man, to which Jewish scholars added a good many footnotes, has been dominated by an acceptance of the definition made by Ranke, a German historian: the task of history is to tell exactly what happened. This Protestant scholarship began in the Enlightenment at the end of the eighteenth and the beginning of the nineteenth centuries. As a consequence, it reflected a rejection of supernatural faith and a scorn of miracles; it held that myth, legend, and true history could be distinguished from each other in general. Protestant scholarship began to apply such distinctions to the materials in the Gospels. Midway in the course of his scholarship, a Britisher, Benjamin Jowett (1817–93), the great translator of Plato, offered the opinion that the Gospels could and should be studied like any other ancient writings; even before Jowett's time this attitude was tacitly assumed by many of the scholars who dealt in the Gospels.

Yet to assert that the Gospels contained anything other than "Gospel truth," that is, to ascribe myth and legend to their contents, was to compromise the traditional Christian position of the divine origin of the Scriptures and to be in conflict with a Fundamentalist Protestant view that the Scriptures are free from any error. The newer scholarship in the nineteenth century emphasized the human aspect of the authorship of the Gospels; indeed, by admitting the possibility of error in the Gospels, many of them came to assume that all of the Gospel material was suspect, unless it was specifically confirmed by non-Gospel materials. While the purpose of the study of the life of Jesus remained religious in the sense that there was sought what one might call "Jesus, a mentor for today," the keynote to the scholarship of the nineteenth century is its iconoclastic character. This scholarship either rejected most of the suppositions of the antecedent Christian tradition as unreliable, or else it addressed itself to the Gospels as if all questions must now be approached anew and without prepossession. It is not possible here to give a full review of that scholarship; this has been done a number of times, and three books and a long article in English are available to anyone wishing an account in greater detail.[1] Yet some of the conclusions of that scholarship should be summarized here.

1.

The usual summaries of modern scholarship on Jesus begin with Hermann Reimarus (1694–1768), a German professor of oriental languages. Of the great deal that Reimarus wrote, two portions were published in 1774 and 1778, through the agency of the German poet and playwright Lessing. The first dealt with resurrection; the second was called, translating its title into English, *Concerning the Purpose of Jesus and His Disciples*. It was Reimarus's view that Jesus viewed the messiahship in its purely Jewish sense, that is, as the human political leader who would break the hold of foreign domination. Jesus hoped to be acclaimed as that Messiah, and he planned his entry into Jerusalem for that purpose, but his effort failed and he was crucified. His disciples stole his body, by stealth; they disseminated the word that Jesus had been resurrected; and they then conceived of Jesus not as a human Messiah, but as superhuman, divine. The mission of this latter Messiah was not to be the political leader, but the redeemer of humanity. In Reimarus's view, all of Jesus' thought was Jewish, his observances were Jewish, his mission was Jewish, and, indeed, the sole difference between Jesus and other Jews was that they believed the

Messiah was still to come, while Jesus believed that he had already come as himself.

Reimarus's view had no immediate effect on scholarship. He is important in that one glimpses in him certain tendencies which were to reappear in subsequent scholarship. First, he insisted on putting Jesus inseparably within a Jewish milieu. Second, the Jewish milieu is that of Jesus' time, not the much earlier age of the prophets of Scripture; the importance here is his emphasis that the Jewish post-biblical literature has a direct importance to the age of Jesus, and the Tanak (the Old Testament) only background importance. Third, he denied all miracles. Fourth, the Jesus who emerges is recognizably human, not superhuman. Fifth, Reimarus, in his construction of history, made use almost exclusively of the Gospels According to Matthew, Mark, and Luke, and very little use of John; [2] we shall presently see that a trend existed of ascribing to John's Gospel no historical worth about Jesus.

In 1822, a Jewish scholar, Isaac Markus Jost (1793–1860), often called the father of modern Jewish historiography, published a nine-volume work, *History of the Israelites from the Time of the Maccabees to Our Age.* He did not ignore Jesus; he recorded laconically some of the data found in the Gospels, but he abstained completely from entering into the questions which were agitating the Christian scholars as to the credibility of the Gospel account. There is, however, some significance in the mere fact that he did not simply ignore Jesus, for thereby he set a precedent for later Jewish historians who were to penetrate more acutely into the questions.

2.

Between the time of Reimarus and 1835, there took place in the world of New Testament learning and lore a broad front of minor storms as skepticism and incredulity whirled about this or that detail in the Gospels, such as the virgin birth, or the exorcism of demons, or Jesus' knowledge of impending events. These storms created some turbulence, but fell short of being a great and convulsing hurricane, for the general public knew little of what was going on in the world of scholars. But in 1835–36, through a publication by a German Lutheran professor of philosophy at the University of Tübingen, the general public became aware of what scholars were doing, and the great storm arose. The man was David Friedrich Strauss; his book was *The Life of Jesus*. Though the book owed debts to precursors, it differed from them in its relative completeness and in its thoroughness. Strauss did not rest content simply to dismiss the miracles in the Gospels as incredible, as his predecessors had done quietly, but he subjected them to a searching examination as to their context in the Gospels and their implications in the Gospel account. Since "accurate history" was his touchstone, Strauss used the word "myth" [3] constantly in characterizing Gospel materials. He was especially alert to reject a view of the miracles, held in his day, which treated them as though they were non-miraculous. In such a view, the narrative that Jesus walked on the water came to be explained that he walked on a sand bar hidden from the sight of his disciples. The motive behind the "rationalizing" of the miracles was to assert the historical reliability of the incident, and to establish its reliability by making it seem not miraculous and not supernatural. Strauss denied that such treatment of the miracles was a responsible one. He preferred to deny the reliability of the incident, rather than merely its supernatural character. A more likely title for Strauss's book could well have been "The Book of Denials." [4]

Strauss denied as mythical the virgin birth, the genealogies which trace Jesus' ancestry to David, the two accounts of Jesus' birth, which Matthew and Luke relate in greatly divergent ways, and even that Bethlehem was the birthplace, the persecution by Herod of Jesus, the flight of the father of Jesus into Egypt, the visit by Jesus to the Temple, the "transfiguration," the resurrection of Jesus—there is little that he affirms.

While the book had two principal defects, the thoroughness of the scholarly work and the unassailable learning which the book reflected made it impossible for those who might have wanted to ignore it to do so. Moreover, the book created a great stir, and promptly went into a succession of editions. The full import of the book can possibly be measured by the results to Strauss; pressure on his university impelled its authorities to dismiss him from his post. The book was, and is, a landmark in the history of Gospel scholarship.

The two defects of the book which I have mentioned are these. First, Strauss was so bent on demonstrating how much of the Gospels was derived from paraphrasing the Hebrew Bible that he seems to have had no perspective on the influence upon the Gospels of the current thought of the age of early Christianity. A certain one-sidedness emerges in his book from an insufficiency of this latter, and by contrast the former is possibly overdone. This can be said in another way, that Strauss so extended the influence of the *remote* Jewish past on Christianity that he did insufficient justice to the role of the developing Church in the creation and shaping of the materials in the Gospels.

The second defect is that Strauss never investigated the very important question of the relationship of the Gospels to each other. This issue can be put in this way, do we have in the four Gospels four quite independent accounts of the events? Or is it possible that one or more Gospels served as a source for the others? What is here at stake, on the first level, is the question of whether we have multiple testimony about Jesus (that is, four different accounts), or, instead, multiple reflections of just one testimony (that is, one account in four versions). If, for example, what Matthew says is something he knew from copying it from Mark, then the agreement of Mark and Matthew on some items represents in reality one voice and not two. Into these questions, significant in Gospel study, Strauss did not enter.[5] A consequence of the failure to enter into the question of literary relationship is that Strauss, for all his keenness in discerning the contradictions and inconsistencies, fell short of discovering the most reasonable and likely way of explaining their bases.

In 1838, a French Jew, Joseph Salvador, son of a Jewish father and a Catholic mother, wrote a book with the title, *Jesus Christ and His Doctrine; the History of the Birth of the Church, Its Organization and Its Progress in the First Century.* Salvador, though a learned man, was not a great scholar. His book is not quite a polemical work, though it borders on it. In brief, he made two points. The first of them is that the difference between the Pharisees and Jesus was that the former conceived of life as susceptible of sanctification, and hence their purpose was to point the way to society for the attainment of the good life. Jesus, on the other hand, had no concern for the needs of society, and was concerned only for the individual; the emphasis on futurity in the teaching of Jesus amounted to a negation of the present. Second, since the Pharisees were concerned for group life, they therefore viewed even religious ceremonies as important; Jesus, on the other hand, according to Salvador, had no interest in those facets of life which relate to the community, and therefore he was unconcerned for the social and ceremonial laws of Judaism. As to the teachings of Jesus, especially the Sermon on the Mount, Salvador was the first of a very long line of Jewish interpreters who have so stressed the conformity of the ethical teachings of Jesus to those of Judaism as to preclude ascribing in this area any originality to Jesus. Salvador regarded Christianity as a blend of both Jewish and pagan elements. This judgment, frequently to be encountered, but especially in Jewish scholars, provides a basis for the latter both to concede that there are indeed Jewish elements in Christendom, and at the same time to emphasize the presence of the non-Jewish; and while this kind of judgment is often only a matter of description, it is also on the borderline of evaluation. More specifically, following this line of scholarship, the Jewishness of Christianity could be conceived as limited to Jesus and his immediate disciples, while the next period, the apostolic age, could be deemed utterly pagan. It would follow, then, that at some stage Christianity had become paganized, but prior to that stage it had been Jewish. One could take the further step, if one cared to, of declaring that earliest Christianity had been not only Jewish, but authentically so, and one could then search for, and naturally find, bases for some affirmative judgment and even some relationship on the part of Jews toward that authentically Jewish basis. In a century in which Protestant scholars were searching for the Jesus of history, Jews in Western lands could enter into the search for what might be called the "Jewish" Jesus. This is the significance of Jost and Salvador.

3.

Respecting the Synoptic problem, that is, the question of the literary relationships of the Gospels, there was revived, in 1838 by a scholar named Weisse, an opinion on the Gospel According to Mark which had been expressed earlier but which had not caught on. This opinion was that Mark was the earliest of the three Synoptic Gospels, Matthew, Mark, and Luke. Thus to regard Mark was to reverse the opinion, dominant for centuries in Christendom, that Mark was a kind of "Reader's Digest" version of Matthew, and was written, of course, later than Matthew. This older view rested on the premise that the author of Matthew was a disciple of Jesus, mentioned in Matthew 9:9; also, the fourth-century Church historian, Eusebius,[6] citing a second-century bishop, Papias, had said that Matthew had recorded in the Hebrew language the words of Jesus and "everyone interpreted them as he was able." The Gospel According to Matthew that has survived to our day is in Greek; if Papias was correct, this Matthew would necessarily be a translation of a document written by an eyewitness in Hebrew. The same Papias had declared that the author of Mark was an interpreter of Peter and that he had recorded in writing [7] all that Peter had remembered of the words and deeds of Jesus. The new opinion that Mark was the earliest of the Gospels arose from the observation that an incident found in all three Gospels is almost invariably longer in Mark than in the other two, and therefore to term Mark an "epitome" of Matthew is clearly impossible, even though Mark's Gospel is shorter than both Matthew and Luke. As to this difference in length, it can be accounted for by the presence in Matthew (and in Luke) of materials (common to Matthew and Luke) which are absent from Mark. This material, common to Matthew and Luke, but absent from Mark, consists mostly of *teachings* ascribed to Jesus; Mark tells pre-eminently what Jesus did, and relatively little about what he taught.

But the theory that Mark was the earliest of the Gospels did not rest simply at the question of which Gospel was written first; the next step was taken in the declaration by scholars that both Matthew and Luke had utilized Mark *as a source* in the composition of their Gospels. Instead of Mark's having omitted or condensed materials found in Matthew, the view now was that Matthew (and Luke) had added to what was in Mark.

It takes but a moment's thought to glimpse some of the inferences which would follow from the view that Matthew and Luke utilized Mark as a source. For one thing, if Matthew used Mark, and in passage after passage copied or rewrote what is in Mark, the great coincidences in the Greek rule out the opinion of Papias that Matthew was originally written in Hebrew, for this is scarcely possible in the case of a Greek writing based on an earlier Hebrew writing. Moreover, if Matthew was based on Mark, then Matthew ceases to be the eyewitness account that it has been held to be, and emerges as a copy of an account which tradition held was written not by an eyewitness but only from an eyewitness' recollections. Second, if Mark is a source for Matthew and Luke, the common testimony of Mark, Matthew, and Luke represents not three bits of testimony, but one bit of testimony and two paraphrases of it. Third, if Mark was the earliest of the Gospels, the presumption could exist that the earliest is synonymous with the most historical. But even Weisse, the scholar who revived the theory of the "priority" of Mark, was unprepared to accept Mark at face value, though Weisse was inclined to attribute a greater measure of reliable history to Mark than to the two later Gospels.

To the question of the non-Marcan material common to Matthew and Luke we shall presently return. We must look now at a relatively new approach to the Gospels with which there is associated a great name in New Testament scholarship, F. C. Baur (1792–1860), who, like Strauss, taught at Tübingen. Baur's main scholarly interest was the history of early Christianity, and particularly in the question, how did it come about that Christianity moved so rapidly and completely from the Jewish into the Greek world? This question of the rapid Hellenization of Christianity has been the focus of many a scholar's work since Baur's day. Baur's answer to the question took the implicit form of rejecting the question, for his answer was that Christianity was *not* quickly Hellenized. He could sustain this view only by declaring that New Testament writings, such as the thirteen Epistles of Paul, were not all of them genuine and therefore not from the very early period; instead, most of the Epistles of Paul were, in his opinion, second-century "pseudographs." Whereas Christian tradition has ascribed infallibility to the Gospels, Baur offered a most radical opinion, namely, that the Gospels were propagandistic essays. The word Baur used was *Tendenz;* it is to be rendered in English as "tendentiousness," in the sense of "partisan," rather than as "tendency." In Baur's mind there was the preconceived notion of how human institutions work, and from the philosopher Hegel he borrowed a pattern, dealing with the reconciliation of opposites (thesis, antithesis, and then synthesis), which he applied to early Christianity. In this view, Jesus was strictly the Jewish Messiah, not the founder of a new religion, and this opinion was held by the disciples Peter and James; so much for "thesis." At the opposite extreme ("antithesis"), Paul held that Jesus was the Messiah of the whole world and that Christianity was distinct from Judaism. These opposite viewpoints clashed for almost a century, according to Baur, but were then reconciled in a sort of colorless Christianity in the second century ("synthesis"). Against this background of interpretation, Matthew's *Tendenz* represented Jewish Christianity; it was relatively more reliable than Mark and Luke, but it had undergone several revisions of the original material to underscore its inherent tendentiousness, and it was not fully reliable historically. Luke represented the Pauline "antithesis," and Mark represented the union, the "synthesis" of the two clashing viewpoints.

Among the difficulties in the viewpoint of Baur was the excessive schematization which forced the New Testament documents to lie on a Procrustean bed, for preconception excessively dominated Baur's conclusions. Yet, on the other hand, this schematization tended to correct a deficiency in David Friedrich Strauss, for it brought into view the likely possibility of the influence of the developing Church in the creation and shaping of the Gospels; Strauss, it will be recalled, had attributed little to the developing Church, ascribing the chief influence to the Hebrew Scriptures. As far as the Jesus of history is concerned, the view of the Tübingen School that the Gospels were "tendentious" added to previous views that they were legendary and theological a further undermining of their historical reliability.[8]

Still another scholar with almost the same name, Bruno Bauer (1809–82), needs to command our attention. Bauer was a vicious Jew-baiter, and active in opposing the wish of German Jews to attain the heights of citizenship. Bauer accepted the view that was growing among scholars that Mark was the earliest of the Gospels. Just as Strauss had implied that "myth" obscured the reliable history in the Gospels, Bauer denied the reliability of much that was in Mark, but still, at one stage of his scholarship, retained the opinion that there had been a historical person named Jesus. At a second stage, however, Bauer moved from the opinion that the Gospel writers had invented incidents into the opinion that they had *invented* Jesus.

4.

At the time that Bruno Bauer was denying there ever was a Jesus, two German Jewish scholars felt that their work in Jewish history confronted them with the need, already encountered by Isaac Markus Jost, to enter into some discussion of Jesus. The first of these was Heinrich Graetz (1817–91) who published an immense, passionate, and learned history of the Jews (1853–75) which has been translated into many languages. What Graetz wrote in his *History* about Jesus he later amplified; this amplification never appeared in German, but was translated into French in 1867 and published under the title *Sinai et Golgotha*. While Graetz's approach to Jesus was rather sympathetic, even warm, he was quite antagonistic to Christianity. This antagonism fell short of the sharp criticism made by eighteenth-century deists of Christians and Christianity (and compared with Kierkegaard's criticism it was almost laudatory), but Graetz was clearly the outsider, and his strictures were resented by some Christians and seemed embarrassing to some of Graetz's own coreligionists. Graetz's criticism of Christianity was not without basis. As to his tone of bitterness, one must concede that there exist among us Jews perceptible strands of bitterness and hostility toward Christians, responses to a history of persecutions, expulsions, and limitations; in Graetz's own lifetime the situation of Jews in Germany was such that he had ample basis for feeling as he did. One remembers what Martin Luther had said: "When I see how Christians have treated the Jews, if I were a Jew, I would rather be a hog than a Christian." [9]

It was Graetz's opinion that since a dominant theme of Christianity is the "renunciation of life," its origin in Judaism is to be linked with the Essenes. That Jewish sect, it will be recalled, was one of the four "philosophies" which Josephus, the first-century Jewish historian, described in the Jewry of that time. Josephus had termed this group to be "Pythagorean," using the phrase so as to convey a quick image to his Gentile readers. The Essenes go unmentioned in both New Testament and rabbinic literature.[10] Yet Graetz leaped to the conclusion that John the Baptist was an Essene, and he therefore saw the Essenes as that segment of Judaism which influenced Jesus and which shaped early Christianity.

While Graetz discounted much of the Gospel account, he still used it, and in a way in which later Jews have used it, namely, accepting the "bare facts," as it were, but diverging from the Gospel interpretation of these "facts." The Jesus found in Graetz's pages is a man who, like the Essenes, "esteemed self-inflicted poverty and despised the mammon of riches." Jesus shared the aversion of the Essenes to marriage; [11] he disavowed oaths. The Essenes, like Jesus, were said to have performed the miraculous exorcism of demons. Jesus, however, did not want his appeal to be lost in the desert as John the Baptist's had been. Moreover, Jesus was well satisfied with the morality of the urban middle classes; therefore he turned his attention "to those who did not belong to, or had been expelled from, the community for their religious offenses, and to the ignorant, poor handicraftsmen and menials." [12]

Graetz went on to apply to the Gospel details his pattern of an Essenelike Jesus appealing to the outcasts of Jewish society. His Jesus was a strict observer of Jewish practice, in every way. His merit, according to Graetz, consisted in "his efforts to impart greater inner force to the precepts of Judaism . . . , in his ardor to make the Judeans turn to God with filial love . . . ; in his insistence that moral laws be placed in the foreground, and in his endeavor to have them accepted by those who had been hitherto regarded as the lowest and most degraded of human beings." The collapse of Jesus' movement in Jerusalem did not lessen the faith in him on the part of what Graetz describes as the unenlightened masses. But the followers were now unwittingly assisted by the Pharisees through their habit of explaining new and marvelous events by interpretation of Scripture. The followers were able to quote passages, especially Isaiah 53, which in their interpretation appeared to predict exactly what Jesus had undergone in that last fateful week in Jerusalem. "His disciples were hourly expecting the return of Jesus [from heaven], and only differed from the Judeans in so far as they thought that the Messiah had already appeared in human form and character."

Graetz moved on to discuss an event, the conversion of a kingdom, Adiabene, to Judaism; at that point he introduced the apostles Paul and Barnabas as two of the Christians who took advantage of a disposition among Gentiles to become Jews by beginning a rival proselytizing movement for the "Nazarene creed." These men, according to Graetz, were obliged to change the original character and purpose of the new movement. Here we see, then, Jewish Christianity giving way to Gentile Christianity.

Graetz's writings show some knowledge of the New Testament, but he came to grips with hardly one of the acute problems raised from within Christianity by the Gospel studies. In his text there is scarcely even an overtone of reflection of David Friedrich Strauss. The question must therefore be asked, why did Graetz write with such confidence in the historical reliability of the Gospel materials even after Strauss had undermined them? Would it not have been expected, rather, that he would espouse Strauss's denials? Why did Graetz see so much history where Strauss saw so little and Bauer none at all? These same questions arise from the work of Geiger.

Abraham Geiger gave a series of lectures, published in 1864, on the theme, *Judaism and Its History*. In them he spoke of Jesus in what one might term a calm and neutral way, abstaining both from praise and from blame. Yet whereas Graetz had called Jesus an Essene, Geiger termed him a "Pharisean Jew with Galilean coloring." Geiger commended the courage and confidence of Jesus; he stated that Jesus uttered no new thought, and he affirmed the Jewishness of Jesus in that he did not "break down the barriers of nationality." Geiger was troubled, however, by the motif of the renunciation of life, for Geiger believed this to be "a morbid principle"; it was not clear to him from the Gospels whether or not this renunciation could be reliably attributed to Jesus. He went on to say that earliest Christianity presented itself not as "a new religion, but affording an impulse for it." This early Christianity was no more than a "belief in the fulfillment of the Messianic hopes as taught by Pharisean Judaism. . . . Whatever else is related concerning the author of Christianity belongs to [the] class of myth." Geiger went on, not to state but merely to imply, that "myth" has resulted in the loss of individual distinctiveness in Jesus, and has "volatilized" him into a mere abstraction.

While Geiger's estimate of Jesus was much briefer than that of Graetz, it had in common with Graetz's an unhesitating recognition of the Jewishness of Jesus. Is it not remarkable that this recognition which ought to be self-evident needed to be arrived at? The fact is that in Christian lore Jesus was regarded as a Christian, and merely to restate that he was a Jew would have the effect of startling people.[13] But to assert the Jewishness of Jesus carried with it the attendant problem: since Christianity ultimately ceased to be a Judaism, at what point did it cease to be Jewish? If this point of cessation was within the lifetime of Jesus, then to assert the Jewishness of Jesus amounted to an empty, even a distorted statement. If this point was after Jesus' lifetime, then a Jewish partisan could simultaneously ascribe the separation of Christianity from Judaism to the intrusion of non-Jewish elements after Jesus' time, and he could proceed to laud the Jewishness of Jesus. He could safely laud, for if Jesus was a Jew, then a Jewish partisan could overcome the centuries-old tradition of scorn, and turn toward praise. Here, then, we must note that Graetz and Geiger had it in common that they tended, as it were, to separate Jesus from Christianity.

I have indicated that neither Graetz nor Geiger espoused the skeptical view of Bauer that Jesus never existed. One cannot know why they did not; one can only speculate. Perhaps they sensed danger to the well-being of German Jews in the effect of Jewish scholars joining in with a radical like Bauer; perhaps Bauer's anti-Semitism repelled them. Perhaps they may have taken a certain pride in Jesus and therefore they did not want to negate his having existed. Yet the likelihood seems to be in a different direction, and to involve a consideration of much greater profundity. It might be phrased in this way: A Jew versed in Scripture and in Talmud who enters into the pages of the Synoptic Gospels finds himself in familiar territory. He can be irked, annoyed, or aghast at the ferocity of the anti-Jewish sentiments, but he is nevertheless in a geography which does not seem strange to him. Scripture is cited in ways like the citations in the Talmud (though, of course, for a very different purpose), the parables of Jesus either duplicate or overlap rabbinic parables, and the "conflicts" which Jesus has with Pharisees and chief priests bring to mind both the animated discussions of the Talmud, and recall intra-Jewish conflicts between Pharisees and Sadducees. Such a Jewish person, for all that he would agree with Strauss that the Gospels are replete with legends and contradictions, would nevertheless hold to the opinion that Gospels and Talmud are similar weavings of similar threads, and such a person would say to a Bauer that no imagination could out of the thin air create so authentically the religious scene and the flavor of Palestinian Judaism. Such a Jew would be prone to say that, however wrong this or that detail of the Gospels may be, the general, over-all impression of a conformity to the general facts is indisputable. To this opinion I myself subscribe.

Yet there is a pitfall in it which may be exemplified in the case of Graetz. So well versed was he in Judaica that apparently he thought that he automatically possessed valid credentials in the Gospels, and he proceeded to express judgments which were never weighed in the light of the accumulated Gospel scholarship and hence judgments which are untenable. His knowledge of Judaism did not lead him to understand the Gospels better, but rather to misunderstand and misinterpret passage after passage.

Strange as it may be, the two Jewish scholars of the time, Graetz and Geiger, were more prone to verify Gospel contents than were Strauss and Bauer. This phenomenon, of Jews being more retentive of Gospel reliability than Christians, was destined to recur.

5.

Geiger had made the point that an accurate understanding of the background of the life and ministry of Jesus was attainable only through a knowledge of the rabbinic literature. It is the word *only* which is the key word in Geiger's statement, for there was other surviving literature from Jewish hands which came from that period. We must here digress at some length to characterize the various types.

First among the non-rabbinic literature are late books which the Greek Jews admitted into their Bible, but the Palestinian Jews did not: I and II Maccabees, Tobit, Judith, and Ecclesiasticus, for example. In the Protestant-Catholic dispute in the sixteenth century, the Protestants had concluded that the authentically sacred books were those ancient ones in the Hebrew Tanak, and for that younger group of writings, found in the Jewish Greek Bible but not in the Hebrew, they used the word "Apocrypha." Since the sixteenth century what we might call the Protestant Bible had differed from the Catholic in that the Catholics consider to be "biblical" certain works which the Protestants label "Apocrypha." The Apocrypha, being late in time of composition, are much closer to the age of Jesus than are the books of the Tanak. But in addition to the Apocrypha, there have survived from the same epoch a number of books which did not gain admission to either the Hebrew or the Greek Bible. This random group of books was assembled and published together only in the eighteenth century. Many of these books carry titles which ascribe their authorship to such Tanak characters as Abraham or Enoch, palpably false ascriptions which led to the use of the word "Pseudepigrapha" ("false titles") as the general name for these books. While many of the Pseudepigrapha, and most of the Apocrypha, were written originally in Hebrew, or in its Semitic first cousin, Aramaic, the surviving copies were mostly in Greek (though some were in Latin or other tongues, such as Ethiopic).

In addition to Apocrypha and Pseudepigrapha, there was a second type of non-rabbinic literature. This is the large heritage from Graeco-Jewish writers, some of it preserved in fragmentary quotation in the Church fathers, but some works surviving in totality. Included in this Graeco-Jewish literature were the writings of Philo [14] (20 B.C.–A.D. 40) and Josephus (A.D. 37/38–105). Philo was a native and resident of Alexandria in Egypt, a city whose Jewish population probably exceeded that of Palestine in the time of Jesus. Philo, though never surpassed in his loyalty to Judaism, was an educated and cultured man, thoroughly at home in the Greek intellectual tradition of Pythagoras, Plato, and the Stoics. A "rationalist," Philo was a profound student of Scripture, though it was the Greek translation, not the Hebrew, in which he worked. From his pen there came a number of works not directly related to Scripture (such as his description, mentioned above, of the Essenes, and another essay describing still another monastic sect, centered in Egypt, called the Therapeutae), but most of his writing was an exposition of some portion of Scripture, principally Genesis and Exodus. His exposition, however, was derived from the manner in which we have come to learn that the Stoics explained Homer. The Stoics used a device called *allegory* ("to say another thing"), and allegory implied that the text was not saying what it seemed to be saying, but saying something quite different. Allegory is a capricious yet useful device, especially in handling passages where the natural meaning is both clear and troubling. For example, Genesis relates that Abraham, at the behest of his wife Sarah, had begotten through Sarah's maid a son, Ishmael. But friction arose between Sarah and Hagar, and therefore Abraham twice drove Hagar from his dwelling, the second time expelling Ishmael also. Philo, troubled by the passage, asserted that Scripture has no interest in portraying the backyard quarrels of two women; what Scripture is relating, so his recourse to allegory assured us, is the conflict between true wisdom (Sarah) and mere schooling (Hagar). With this allegory controlling his approach to the narrative of Abraham, Sarah, and Hagar, he wrote a very fine essay on the merits, but the limitations of, shall we say, the liberal arts tradition; the name of the essay is "Concerning Mating for the Sake of Erudition"—a reflection of Philo's conviction that the true meaning of Abraham's mating with Hagar was his matriculation in the liberal arts.

The convenience of allegory to Philo was such that he was enabled to read into the Tanak his vast Greek erudition—and to believe that he was reading this erudition out of Scripture. So much a Platonist was he (a Church father said that either Plato Philonizes or Philo Platonizes) that he raised for himself the question of the relationship of Moses and Plato, who he concluded were in essence saying the same thing. To his question, Philo gave the answer (subsequently repeated by the Church fathers) that Plato derived, that is, plagiarized, his teachings from Moses.

Philo's writings assist in the comprehension of Paul and John. The Epistle to the Hebrews is so quasi-Platonic that Philo's Platonism is most useful there also. Moreover, Philo's dates—his lifetime overlapped those of Jesus and of Paul—would naturally give him a special relevancy from that standpoint alone. No study of the merger of Jewish or Christian doctrines of revelation with Greek philosophy is complete without some attention to this first major blending of the heritages.

Whereas Philo's importance is in the realm of theology and philosophy, that of Josephus, whose writings are also in Greek, is primarily in history. His *Antiquities of the Jews* not only recounted biblical history, with many imaginative or romantic additions, but he carried his account down beyond the biblical period and into his own time; Josephus is virtually our only historical source for the late period of Jesus. A second work, *The Jewish Wars,* is our richest source for the tumultuous events in Palestine which culminated in the disastrous rebellion against Rome in A.D. 66–70. Josephus was far from a reliable historian— he was an apologist, a propagandist, rather than a modern historian—but without Josephus we would be almost bereft of information, for example, about such people who figure in the Gospels as Herod the Great and Herod Antipas; Josephus tells us about both John the Baptist and about James the brother of Jesus. I quoted above, on pages 17–18, the disputed passage which mentions Jesus.[15] Yet even if it is admitted that the passage is interpolated, Josephus is still invaluable for the history and somewhat for the thought of Jews in the first Christian century.

That the Apocrypha, Pseudepigrapha, Philo, Josephus, and other less important writings are in Greek means that they are in the same language as the New Testament and hence their contents readily susceptible to study by the New Testament specialist.

The rabbinic literature, to return now to Geiger, is in Hebrew and Aramaic, and represents a field of study for which arduous preparation is required. It is immense in quantity. In style it is both terse and yet replete with allusiveness, and both factors make it difficult to comprehend. Moreover, it is technical, for it was the compiled answers to questions of meticulous Jews concerning religious law, and therefore it presupposes on the part of the reader an abundance of quite technical knowledge. At a number of stages in the Renaissance and in the rise of Humanism, Christian scholars made anthologies of rabbinic literature which they translated into Latin; a New Testament scholar could, as it were, have access to excerpts, merely excerpts, in these translations. Some difficulties with these excerpts escaped both the compilers and the users. First, the excerpted material entered the anthology only if it seemed to impinge on the New Testament, with the result that the excerpts answered the implied question, what bearing does the rabbinic literature have on New Testament? and not the important prior question, what is it that the rabbinic literature is saying? Citations devoid of context are always dangerous; one can "prove atheism by Scripture." (There is a passage, in Psalm 14:1, which says, "There is no God"; the whole passage reads, "The fool has said in his heart that there is no God.") What the somewhat knowledgeable excerpter provided and what the novice inferred from this provision of rabbinic material could well be as different as night from day. Second, the quintessence of the spirit of rabbinic literature could lie quite outside the excerpted passages, and the novice could be misled into supposing that he knew the spirit when he was in reality only on the periphery. Third, the man who deals only in excerpts necessarily lacks that mastery which alone provides a personal sense of authority. Fourth, since the rabbinic literature is difficult (and the mere translation of it is in reality only the prelude to understanding it), the texts have, for the most part, gone without scientific editing or scientific commentary, even today.

There were, then, the two bodies of Jewish materials available to the scholar: on the one hand, the Apocrypha and Pseudepigrapha and the Hellenistica in Greek, and on the other hand, the rabbinic literature in Hebrew and Aramaic. The smoother road for the scholar who knew Greek was the first body, and therefore the vast majority of the New Testament scholars abstained from personally traveling the second, the rocky road. What Geiger was saying, however, was that the genuine understanding of the New Testament as related to Judaism should come from the second body, for the first was, to his mind, not nearly as close or nearly as focused. Geiger did not make an additional point that others were to make later, that the rabbinic literature was preserved and transmitted by Jews, whereas the Graeco-Jewish literature was the legacy of Christendom and unknown to Jews until the age of Humanism. The term "normative" was to arise to characterize the rabbinic literature, with its natural implication that the other was marginal, peripheral. Geiger's strictures did not immediately affect Christians, but in the wake of his view of the proximity of rabbinic literature and the Gospels to each other, there arose a constantly increasing stream of publications, as Jewish scholars used their knowledge of rabbinics to write explanations of phrase after phrase in the New Testament. So voluminous has this output been in the past one hundred years that it defies summary here. This flood of writing included rivulets that were muddy and some that were crystal clear, and it included both the earnest and the thorough, and also the merely ingenious. (It must also be confessed that in some of this writing an occasional scholar, confident that he was teaching Christians about their Scriptures, wrote in spectacular misunderstanding of the given New Testament passage.) Although most of this writing has consisted of unconnected bits and pieces, it has proved to be valuable scholarship. Only gradually did Jews begin to imitate the precedent of Salvador and devote a whole book to Jesus or to the Gospels; possibly more would have done so had they not been deterred by what seemed forbidden territory, as though the explication of some single phrase was not so great a trespass as a whole book.

A Frenchman, Ernest Renan, wrote his book, *The Life of Jesus*, in 1863. He stated in his introduction that Geiger was right in contending that the rabbinic literature is relevant to Christianity, and he wrote that he had verified in the texts themselves every passage he used; he mentioned a Jew named Neubauer who assisted him in checking these passages. The instance of Renan and Geiger was the first to my knowledge of some scholarly exchange between a Christian and a Jew on the topic of Jesus. Geiger was very critical of Renan's book, but on a basis quite other than the use or non-use of rabbinic literature.

Renan's *Life of Jesus* is quite unlike Strauss's. The German scholar's book is completely devoid of narrative, and consists, instead, of a detailed discussion of incident after incident in the Gospels, and is devoted to deciding whether that incident was historical or not. Renan's book reads like a novel. Only in the brief introduction did Renan discuss matters of scholarly import; while he gave footnotes to support his conclusions, he did not let us see into his mind, as Strauss did, nor did he tell us how the conclusion was reached. Strauss's book is cold, analytical, and negative; Renan's is warm, imaginative, and, despite the denial of this or that detail, affirmative.

Renan's Jesus is as thoroughly naturalistic and human as any great hero in a novel. It is a glowing account, a work of adulation and almost of adoration. Its denials, especially of much of the contents of the Gospel According to John, called forth from pious Christians a stream of invective comparable to that engendered by Strauss's book. Renan had been born and bred a Roman Catholic, and had begun to study for the priesthood, but religious skepticism had impelled him to withdraw. He embarked on studies in Semitic languages and history, and became a scholar of good reliability and training. France, then as now, was a Catholic country in which a sizable portion of the middle and upper classes maintained either a loose and nominal connection with the Church or none at all. For this literate portion of the population, Renan's *Life of Jesus* was a most welcome event; its skepticism, and its easy scholarship, may well have persuaded them that they already knew what he was telling them, and it provided the impression that the approach of Renan was a sanction for the non-Church Christianity that they suddenly discovered they espoused. The extravagant praise of Renan's book in these circles increased the sense of outrage on the part of both Catholic and Protestant religious conservatives, with the usual consequence that a disputed book gains readers often as much from the dispute as from its own qualities.

In the scholarly world Renan was taken to task in the learned tomes of his time for two major transgressions. The first of these was that he had given insufficient attention to the Gospel problem, the Synoptic problem; as a consequence some of his judgments ran counter to the emerging consensus among the German researchers. The second transgression was, for scholars, that he had not specified the objective criteria by which he could justify his acceptance of some items as historical and others as not. For example, he denied that the discourses in John were authentically by Jesus, yet he accepted the pattern of incidents in John as reliable. To scholars the issue was not so much whether he was right or wrong, but that he made no effort, such as Strauss had made, to set forth some guiding principles for these decisions. Without these principles his conclusions seemed to be capricious, despite the elaborate learning which his book disclosed.

Geiger's criticism of Renan overlapped that of the conservative Christian scholars in alleging inconsistency and caprice, but Geiger proceeded to take Renan to task for seeming to set Jesus over and against Judaism rather than within it.[16] But he went on to still another facet of the first criticism, and, as David Friedrich Strauss had written a second Life of Jesus at this same time, a book which was narrative and affirmative, Geiger included Strauss in this facet of his criticism. What disturbed Geiger was the ability of Renan to be so negative toward the Gospels as historical documents, and at the same time so affirmative toward their assessment of Jesus. Since Geiger's estimate of Jesus had been respectful but hardly enthusiastic, it may be that he reflected what is possibly instinctive among us Jews, namely, the tendency to withhold ourselves from extravagant praise of Jesus, for we never go beyond regarding him as one more good man in the long history of good men, and in that line we do not place him as pre-eminent. The scholarly world was destined to see endless repetitions of the spectacle Renan presented, namely, the New Testament scholar who rejects the historical worth of most of the Gospel materials, but who seems able to muster a Life of Jesus in which he appears to have forgotten his own denials.

Geiger attacked Renan on this score. Yet what Renan did ought not to be scorned as mere inconsistency (so it appears to me), but needs to be seen in the light of two important factors. The first, a complicated one, owes its origin to the influence of the same Hegel whose philosophy influenced both Baur and Strauss. Within that philosophy there was a conception of the "absolute" idea, or "absolute" spirit, and Christianity was regarded as the incarnation of the absolute philosophy, which could and would develop into the absolute religion, and Jesus was the ideal man in that philosophy. In this light the depiction of Jesus in Strauss's second book, and in that of Renan, is not a creation of mere personal caprice, however capricious it may seem, but is rooted in a metaphysical system which to its adherents seemed true and right. In the light, then, of such an antecedent conditioning, Renan could at the same time slash away at the reliability of the Gospel materials about Jesus and still conceive of him as the ideal man, and then revert to judiciously selected materials in order to document Jesus as the ideal.

But there is also a second factor which eludes ready grasp by us Jews. In our way, we are prone not to regard the person, but only his words; our prayer books cite from the prophets, the Psalms, the rabbinic literature, but they do not mention the persons whose words are cited, nor, of course, glorify that person. Indeed, in rabbinic literature the formula whereby a scriptural verse is quoted reads simply "as it is written," or "for it is said," without specifying which particular scriptural book is being quoted. Only in relatively modern times, when an interest in history was awakened, have we become aware of persons to the point of interesting ourselves in them as individuals. This interest, however, relates to history, and not to our prayer book, for in the latter we continue to concentrate on words, not on persons. While we have had high estimates of the relative worth of famous persons, and have ascribed a certain pre-eminence to Abraham, Moses, Hillel, Maimonides, these to us represent men of eminence, even of special eminence, but never to the point that we lose the sense of that humanity which they share with us and we with them. We have never considered greatness to have to be interchangeable with perfection, and therefore we are not dismayed by the accounts in Scripture of the human defects in an Abraham, a Moses, or a David. Even in our partisanship for these names which come onto our tongues in our early childhood, we have never ascribed to them an eminence sealed off in principle from our own attainment, for we think of them as circumscribed by human limitations comparable to, though greatly less than, the limitations which circumscribe us; in admiring their attainments we are telling ourselves that it is not ruled out that we too can attain to their greatness.

This tendency is quite the reverse of the Christian view of Jesus, and it is just as much the reverse of the view of Christian iconoclastic scholars of Jesus as it is of the pre-modern view of

Christians. A reading of the various books called "The Life of Jesus" leads the reader to the inevitable conclusion that there is often very little correlation between the denials of the scholar of this or that detail in the Gospel and the intuitive determination to see in Jesus the "ideal man." It is not the case that scholarly or critical principles are withheld, but the case is rather that these principles which might have moved a Jewish reader to expect some radically reduced assessment of Jesus never result in such a reduction. In the iconoclastic scholarship only Jesus himself remains free from equation with other humans; a Paul, a Peter, or even Mary become subject to such equation. Indeed, Paul is periodically dismissed, even by Christians, as an arrogant epileptic who distorted the teachings of Jesus, or a Peter's primacy satirized in works hostile to the Catholic adulation of him, or the Mariology of the Catholics scorned as Mariolatry, but the person of Jesus never undergoes such irreverence; the pedestals of Mark, Matthew, Luke, and John are often shaken but Jesus remains to such irreverent scholars a constant object of their reverence.

To Geiger, and to later Jewish writers, this anomaly of abiding reverence in the midst of ruthlessly negative scholarship appeared inconsistent, as one might well expect. Yet one must comment that a certain naïveté is evident in Geiger's expecting what he should never have expected. In the minds of Christians the person of Jesus is so central as to be immune to the logic and even the data of scholarship; and while the Jesus of both the Unitarians and of the "unitarians" within Protestant denominations supposedly is a man and no more than a man, he is there conceived of as the supreme man of all history. While on the level of articulate presentation there is a manifest difference between the divine Christ and a human Jesus, still on the inarticulate level the difference is blurred, and the margin of difference almost evanescent. The error of Geiger was that of imputing to such as Renan an unreserved and unlimited carrying through of scholarship and logic; Geiger was quite unprepared to discover that intuitive imagination was even stronger in Renan than pure scholarship.

As to Bruno Bauer, who denied that there ever was a Jesus, Bauer's book, *Philo, Strauss, Renan and Primitive Christianity,* published in 1874, summarized his earlier views. Bauer was no ignoramus, and his writings exhibit his deep and broad learning, and also his prejudices. He knew Philo well; he was only dimly aware of rabbinic literature. We said above that Philo's *Logos* and the *Logos*-Christ of the New Testament were links in the same religious, theosophical chain. Bauer contended that Renan and Strauss had completely misunderstood the sequence of developments in early Christianity, for they, in isolating a human Jesus from New Testament legends and theology, supposed that the order of the process was from the man Jesus into a divine being. According to Bauer, the process was exactly the reverse, and what happened was not that a man became progressively more and more deified, but that an abstraction, Philo's *Logos*, came to be more and more humanized, and that out of this progressive humanization there emerged a man Jesus who had never really lived. There is this measure of aptness in Bauer's view, that in the early Church there was agreement that Jesus was divine, and the quarrels then were on his humanity, affirmed by most but denied by many. But Bauer marshaled his evidence one-sidedly, and he did not do justice to the counterbalancing evidence.

However near to each other are the denial of the reliability of the Gospel account and the denial that there ever was a Jesus, it must be emphasized that these two viewpoints are the opposites of each other. One could affirm, as Strauss and Baur had done, that the Gospels as documents were a melange of legends, theology, and tendentiousness which concealed Jesus (rather than revealing him), but at the same time assert that behind and beyond the legends there stood a historical man. The denial that there ever was a Jesus is quite a different thing, for it would imply that the Gospels do not reflect a normal growth and development from a historical person to unhistorical legends and beliefs about him, but that it was all put together out of the whole cloth, and represents simply a tissue of falsity. Bauer was too well trained a scholar to rest his negative case on mere assertion, and therefore he felt it necessary to give what he considered a more persuasive view of the true nature of the Gospels than did his opponents, and also he felt it necessary to break down their case. This latter especially would seem to have appealed to him and he gave himself to the task both in highly technical writing and also in the more popular book named above.

Bauer remains a curiosity. The importance of his denial that Jesus ever lived may help in underlining the assertions of many scholars concerning the unreliability of the Gospel tradition, for it is not too long a stride across the boundary between denying that the Gospels are historical and that Jesus ever lived. Bauer took that step because the real boundary line was obscured from him through prepossession. In our context it is worthy of note that at the same time that Renan and the later Strauss depicted a Jesus at variance with Judaism, and Bauer was denying there ever was a Jesus, Graetz and Geiger were asserting the authenticity of the Jewishness of Jesus.

6.

The march of scholarship which had criticized Strauss and Renan for failing to consider the relationship of the Gospels to each other proceeded to develop what is called the "two source" hypothesis. We have mentioned the growth of the opinion that Matthew and Luke had each utilized Mark; in the "two source" hypothesis, one of these two sources is Mark. As to the second source, we have already seen that Mark concentrated on incident, and that in both Matthew and Luke the greater length consisted of a large quantity of material which depicted Jesus as teaching. This common material is present, undeniably; in Matthew it is assembled into blocks; in Luke it is scattered throughout the Gospel. How did the two Gospels come to contain this common material? Three optional explanations existed. Perhaps Matthew drew his material from Luke, or perhaps Luke drew it from Matthew, or perhaps both Matthew and Luke drew it from a source which no longer exists. Scholars have espoused all three explanations, but by far the largest number fixed on the third. The German word for source is *Quelle;* this source is usually referred to as Q. Mark and Q are the two sources, then, in the "two source" hypothesis.

Just as Mark, to have been available to Matthew and Luke,

must have been earlier than they, so too Q needed to be earlier. To the usual mind, earlier has meant more historically reliable; indeed, one could proceed, in the light of supposed *early* sources and the *late* use of them, to a gradation in the reliability of the materials. The total negations of the early Strauss and the caprices of Renan gave way subsequently to an actual reassessment by scholars of the historical problem. Their examination of the Gospels and their interrelations, positive and negative, was pursued both with great vigor and with meticulous care, and one can say in admiration of the thoroughness of the magnificent scholarship that no possible avenue was left unexplored. The fundamental issue remained what it had been, how can we isolate the Jesus of history? Monograph followed monograph in endless profusion, and the writing of a Life of Jesus on the basis of the unfolding scholarship seemed the inescapable task of every eminent New Testament scholar. These scholarly "lives" were works of carefulness and of an effort at objectivity. The one common criticism to make of them was that the man Jesus whom they described was a blend of the ideal man and, at the same time, the reflection of the image of the nineteenth-century scholar who was writing about him. Since the occasional Jew who now wrote about Jesus was a citizen of the Western World, the Jesus whom such a Jew recreated bore a comparably striking resemblance to his author.[17]

A difficulty which plagued the Christian authors of the books on a human Jesus was their need to specify some unique human achievement on his part. The growth of the body of rabbinic learning related to Jesus had documented beyond easy refutation the similarity of the teachings of Jesus to the teachings of the Jews of his day, except for those passages which dealt with his supernatural role. The parables of Jesus duplicated rabbinic parables, especially when Christian scholars [18] pared these down from their extended, allegorical form into what seemed to be the basic parable. Even on the part of those scholars who contrasted an ideal man and fallible rabbis, the similarity of the teaching was undeniable. But a way out of his Jewish net was found. It rested in attributing to Jesus one of the contributions of Paul, this by a double distortion.

Nineteenth-century scholars were sufficiently influenced by eighteenth-century rationalism to adopt an approach to Paul which often fell little short of disparagement. It was concluded, for example, that Paul was an epileptic, that he and not Jesus was responsible for the supernatural opinions about Jesus, and hence that Paul was the prime source of all that modern man had basis for objecting to in Christianity. While the orthodox strove to find some bond to tie Jesus and Paul to each other, the unorthodox played them off in such a way that the stereotyped non-scholarly view arose that just as Jesus was the hero of the Christian epic, Paul was its villain. There circulated a poem:

> A Jew named Saul,
> Later called Paul,
> Came and spoiled it all.

One of Paul's distinctive contributions—which makes him always uncongenial to Jews—is his contention that the Laws of Moses cannot bring a man to righteousness, but in fact impede him, and hence they are nullified. This criticism by Paul of the Law, a reluctant but unreserved criticism, was reshaped a bit in the Gospel scholarship and ascribed now to Jesus, and the Law and its supposed effect on Jews was reshaped so as to provide the basis for that criticism which it was imagined that Jesus had made.

All this was consistent with the motif in Renan, that Jesus was over and against the Judaism of his time. There was constructed in Gospel scholarship a Judaism which Jesus would naturally have opposed (just as I and other Jews would oppose it). It was derived not from a misunderstanding of rabbinic Judaism, but from falling short of understanding it. The rabbinic literature is largely a library centered on the biblical laws and their observance and interpretation, so that it has a natural legal, and admittedly legalistic, tone. But the lawyer's library by no means exhausts the literature of the Jews, for Jews have their prayer book and they have the Psalms and the Prophets. And, above all, the legalistic literature itself contains copious passages of an edifying character.[19] Nevertheless, the Christian scholars evolved a view of Judaism which attributed to it the character of a legalism and nothing but a legalism. I lamented in an article [20] that the Christian scholarship normally alluded to not a dry or an arid legalism, but a dry *and* arid legalism; I was quite surprised to read in the *Interpreter's Bible Dictionary* (which was published in 1962 and to which I and some dozen other Jews contributed) a new phrase for it, dry and *sterile*.[21] The Law was held to be, and seems still to be interpreted as, a burden, a yoke, under which Jews groaned; it seemed never to occur to such interpreters that what is a privilege to carry never seems a burden to those who bear it. Such scholars saw Judaism as no more than a system of rewards and punishments, these for observing or failing to observe the externals of religion; Jews had sunk from the great heights of the pre-exilic prophets into rabbinic legalism so that they had lost sight of the heart of religion. Along such lines there was depicted the Judaism into which Jesus was born.

The human contribution of Jesus, so it was alleged, was to restore the heart to religion. Passages previously troublesome now lent themselves to ready solution: Matthew had depicted Jesus as saying that he came not to annul the Law but to fulfill it, and the Sermon on the Mount is a series of seven increases of the Laws of Moses into a greater legal severity. A scholar, predetermined to view Judaism as the legalism with which Jesus broke, could now misinterpret these passages into meaning that Jesus substituted *intent* and *basic attitude* for the Law itself, for legalism was so bad that Jesus needed shielding from embracing it.

How could serious scholars allow themselves to be beguiled into this double distortion, despite their scholarship? The answer goes beyond merely attributing to them blind prepossession and must assume that they knew rabbinic Judaism only from the anthologies in Latin, or only from the citations of it in New Testament commentaries.[22]

I must here not be misunderstood. Were I an Orthodox Jew, I could be charged with arguing *pro domo*. I am a Reform Jew for whom the rabbinic legalism elicits no more than antiquarian interest. Perhaps my Jewish ancestry is here offended; that may well be the case, but if so, it is on an instinctive, unconscious level. On the conscious level, it is the pedant in me who is offended, for

I hold that neither the role of Jesus nor the nature of Judaism is at all properly described and evaluated in these contrasts between Jewish legalism and Jesus' intent. Such scholarship tended to separate Jesus from Judaism in a way counterbalancing Graetz and Geiger, who tended to separate him from Christianity.

7.

Lives of Jesus continued to be written in the nineteenth century, but never with any definitiveness. The example of Renan, that of capricious selection and exclusion, prompted one scholar after another to write a supposedly more reliable book than that of the scholar whose work the new book was expected to replace. The best characterization of these books can be found by leaping a little ahead, to 1900, when a great scholar of New Testament and Church history, Adolf von Harnack, gave a series of lectures in Berlin. The translation of the German title of the lectures is "The Essence of Christianity"; the title of the English translation is *What Is Christianity?* To Harnack, Christianity was "something simple and sublime; it means one thing and one thing only. Eternal life in the midst of time, by the strength and under the eyes of God." Harnack ruled out of Christianity the Catholic Church, ecclesiasticism, doctrine, dogma, the authority of persons, and even a concern with the problems of society. As to Jesus, Harnack said not one word about the virgin birth, the atoning death, or the resurrection. He said that Jesus never attended a rabbinical school, nor was he an Essene, but a man who "lived in religion, and whose whole life, all his thoughts and feelings, were absorbed in the relation to God."

That Harnack's view represented the extreme in capricious selection and exclusion was quickly demonstrated in a book called, in its English translation, *The Gospel and the Church,* by a Frenchman, Alfred Loisy. The latter was then a Catholic priest. His attack on Harnack took the form of insisting that the Church could not be disregarded in any effort to understand Christianity; even the Gospels, so said Loisy, were not so much documents about Jesus as creations by the Church which shaped the Gospels in the light of Church experience, need, and belief.[23] In a word, Loisy accused Harnack of fashioning Christianity in the light of his own dispositions and preferences.

The mentality of Harnack can be taken as somewhat typical of those late-nineteenth-century scholars who wrote scholarly Lives of Jesus. Not that their learning was small; to the contrary. Not that they had a deliberate bias against Jews or Judaism; they often had an even stronger bias against Roman Catholicism. Their construction of a Jesus who restored the heart to an arid Judaism was no more than a reflection of their own view, the supposition of which they never thought of challenging, that Jesus was, anachronistically, a nineteenth-century German scholar whose religion was something simple and sublime. The Jewishness of Jesus was almost totally absent from Harnack, and the various Lives of Jesus, the latest contradicting the previous, managed to put Jesus into a Jewish setting and still immunize him from Judaism.

The protest of Jews, especially to Harnack, was quite vocal, though not nearly so much as was the protest of orthodox Christians. For Jewish scholars, there arose, unobserved, the dilemma that, in order to combat the view which incorrectly separated Jesus from Judaism, they were forced to assert all the more strongly his Jewishness. Jewish writings not only proclaimed the Jewishness of Jesus, but began to express a kinship with him. Such writers began to reclaim Jesus for Judaism, and then some of them, as we shall see, began to reclaim Jesus for the Jewish community.

The various Lives of Jesus written before Harnack's lectures are customarily referred to as "liberal," this in the sense opposite to conservative, and they merit the adjective in the freedom which the authors felt to express a personal judgment on thorny questions, untrammeled by traditional preconceptions. The freedom could seem to its opponents to be mere license, and restraints could seem to be absent. Discontented as I am with the combination of caprice and anachronisms in those works, and offended as I have felt at their frequently shabby disparagement of Judaism, I feel impelled to defend them from one standpoint, namely, that they represented earnestly the fullest attainable intellectual honesty. These were not superficial books, nor sycophantic, nor consciously biased, and if one moves from one of these books to another and notes the often picayune character of the criticism which the authors made of each other, one ought to recognize that the liberal scholarship contained within itself the potential of self-criticism, and the very freedom of the authors committed them to this self-search. While on the one hand the authors were carrying on a tradition, on the other it was a tradition of the right of free inquiry, and their honest and admirable dedication to free inquiry was a valid safeguard against the development of a liberal "orthodoxy." It was inevitable that their anachronisms and errors would come to be pointed out; it was inevitable that the Protestant scholars themselves would come to see the deficiencies in their treatment of Judaism; it was inevitable that the entirety of the liberal tradition would come to be questioned, and from within.

8.

In 1892 a scholar named Johannes Weiss (1863–1914) published a small book, *Die Predigt Jesus vom Reiche Gottes,* which would be translated "Jesus' Preaching about the Kingdom of God." Indirectly it was a powerful protest against the projections whereby Jesus was portrayed as if he were a citizen of the nineteenth century. Weiss drew attention to what is called "eschatology" in the teaching of Jesus. Eschatology is the name given to the motif in the ancient Jewish and Christian literature which deals with what is to happen at the end of time; the phrase, "Repent for the kingdom of God is at hand," and other passages have some relationship to eschatology. To repeat what we have said above, the Jewish view of the advent of the Messiah was conceived of as ushering in either the end of time or at least the beginning of some new epoch to replace the current one. In the Christian conception, as we have said, the pattern involved two steps. The first of these, merely preparatory, was Jesus' appearance on earth, and the second and climactic step would be his return from heaven where he had ascended after his resurrection. There are passages in the Gospels, then, which clearly quote Jesus as expecting the eschatological moment of the end of time in the nearest future.

Whatever may have been the substance of this expectation, it did not come about. While the Christian denominations have not abandoned mention of the second coming, the view is scarcely a vivid one, and the established and settled Churches have paid virtually no attention to it. Accordingly, the liberal scholars tended totally to ignore this motif in the Gospels, especially since there are Gospel passages which seem to reflect the opinion that the kingdom of God was not something for the future, but had already been ushered in at the first coming of Jesus. Furthermore, in at least one passage, (Luke 17:21) "the kingdom of God is within you," the idea is "spiritualized" through making it an individual, personal matter.[24] The explanation given for the variety of views in the New Testament is that Jesus had originally preached and expected the climactic moment, and so had the Church; but as the years went on and the moment failed to arrive, its futurity underwent the alterations noted. Yet despite the alterations in the transmission of his words, the tradition nevertheless seems to point persistently to Jesus' having preached the early end of the world; Jesus' preachment that the kingdom of God was near and would soon come was of no great consequence in the liberal Lives of Jesus. When Weiss emphasized that Jesus had expected and had preached the early end of the epoch, then in effect he was denying the validity of a nineteenth-century Christian Jesus, and insisting, instead, on a first-century Jewish Jesus. So persuasive was Weiss's book that it presaged the end of the liberal Lives of Jesus.

That end was hastened by a book published in 1901 which owed a debt to Weiss, but chose a curious way of paying it. The author was Wilhelm Wrede, and the book was *Das Messiasgeheimnis in den Evangelien*, "The Messianic Secret in the Gospel." Wrede noted that on the one hand some passages in Mark present Jesus as the Messiah, and on the other hand many passages portray Jesus as keeping secret his Messianic character.

Wrede was persuaded that the latter passages were false and incongruous, and he went on to aver that the Jesus of history was a simple teacher who never made the claim to be the Messiah; the passages which depict him as the Messiah were the later product of the faith of the disciples. In effect, Wrede was saying that Jesus is portrayed in Mark as keeping secret a role which he had never claimed. Weiss's insistence on eschatology in the message of Jesus came in Wrede's treatment to be the eschatology of the disciples, not Jesus' own. As to the broader implication of Wrede's theory, it was this, that adherents of the "two source" hypothesis were accustomed to consider Mark as the earliest, and hence the most historical of the Gospels; now they were being challenged by the contention that Mark itself was minimally historical.

Albert Schweitzer, born in 1875, the venerable medical missionary and authority on Bach, came to fame through a book he wrote in 1906. Its English translation bore the title *The Quest of the Historical Jesus;* the German title was *Von Reimarus zu Wrede* ("From Reimarus to Wrede"). The book was primarily an extended review of the scholarship on the life of Jesus encompassed in the period between these two men, especially the German, Protestant scholarship. Of the Jesus of the liberal biographies, Schweitzer had this to say (in the English translation, p. 396): "There is nothing more negative than the result of the critical study of the life of Jesus. The Jesus of Nazareth who came forward publicly as the Messiah, who preached the ethic of the Kingdom of God, who founded the Kingdom of Heaven upon earth, and died to give his work its final consecration, never had any existence. He is a figure designed by rationalism, endowed with life by liberalism, and clothed by modern theology in an historical garb."

Schweitzer, in rejecting the Jesus of the liberal scholars, made a proposal of his own. With Johannes Weiss, he emphasized the eschatology in the teaching of Jesus, but he believed that that eschatology dominated not just the teaching of Jesus, but the whole of Jesus' life and the whole of Jesus' awareness.

The extension of eschatology beyond a teaching matter can

appear to an outsider like me to be a matter of fluent words without any real meaning, and when this view is applied to the Gospels, it can seem to be every bit as capricious as the liberal Lives which Schweitzer was rejecting in order to suggest his own supposedly more reliable view. But even if one were to concede that Schweitzer's "thoroughgoing" eschatology validly represents what is in the Gospels, then the end result would appear to an outsider as a magnificently conceived dead-end street. This is so because to emphasize eschatology means necessarily to underscore the teaching ascribed to Jesus that the end of the world was soon to come, and if Jesus taught that, he was mistaken, as Protestant scholars have stated openly. One wonders, then, at the selection of an item such as this as the principal clue to the otherwise elusive Jesus of history, and one wonders even more at recent Gospel scholarship which retains as historical only Jesus' eschatology.

To the Jesus of the liberal Lives, a Jew would possibly have some relationship, but the Jesus of thoroughgoing eschatology would underscore the opinion of Geiger and Graetz that Jesus was a "renouncer of life," and while such a tendency is found at times and places in Jewish history, it was never more than occasional, random, and marginal. One might say that the previous liberal scholars were fashioning a Jesus to whom Jewish scholars could come progressively closer, but that Schweitzer's conclusions served to diminish the growing proximity.[25] While we shall see the opinions of two Jews in just a moment, we must understand even at this point that these two, Montefiore and Klausner, reflected the pre-Schweitzer scholarship, however much after Schweitzer they wrote.

In addition to Schweitzer, the bankruptcy of the liberal Lives of Jesus as unhistorical creations of the liberal mind was set forth from a quite different viewpoint by a Swiss scholar, Peter Schmiedel, in an exhaustive article, "Gospels," in the *Encyclopaedia Biblica*, published in 1901. In the third section of his article, Schmiedel dealt with the credibility of the Gospels. After denying the credibility of almost all of the materials, Schmiedel came to the conclusion that certainly five, and possibly an additional four, passages are absolutely credible. What makes these passages credible is that they contain sentiments which go against the grain of developing Church adulation. Thus, for Jesus to have rejected being called good—"Why do you call me good? None is good but God alone" (Mark 10:18)—would not have been dreamed up by the Church, and therefore it is credible. So too are the passage which relates that his relatives thought him insane (Mark 3:21); the passage in which only God—God and not Jesus—knows when the end of the epoch is to come (Mark 13:32); the words on the cross, "My God, my God, why have you forsaken me"; and the willingness of Jesus to forgive blasphemy against him, but not against the Holy Spirit. These five passages, according to Schmiedel, "might be called the foundation pillars for a truly scientific life of Jesus." If Schmiedel were right, then the liberal Lives, which conservatives in the nineteenth century regarded as excessively skeptical, would turn out to be excessively credulous. Schmiedel represents an extreme viewpoint, not a middle-of-the-road opinion; yet there is a sense in which his negative conclusions are only somewhat more numerous than the negativism to be found in some one single book. If one were to tot up the negative conclusions of all the liberal Lives, these would outnumber Schmiedel's, for Schmiedel was not so much asserting that the Jesus of history could not be scientifically recovered as that the efforts had been deficient.

Yet the negativism of Schmiedel and of Schweitzer was mild compared with the revival around the turn of the century of Bruno Bauer and the denial that there ever had been a Jesus. That thin line between denying the reliability of the inherited information about Jesus and the assertion that he never lived became a kind of fixed point around which revolved some men who in one part of the ambit denied what was in the Gospels but at the other part denied there ever was a Jesus. While such deniers were to be found in Holland and in France, the three leading names are those of the Englishman John M. Robertson, the German Arthur Drews, and the American mathematician William B. Smith. Whereas Bruno Bauer had based his denial that Jesus ever lived on his understanding of the religious-theosophical writings of the age, the bases of these later deniers—insofar as they had bases—were derived from the study of comparative religion, a discipline which was then coming into its own, especially in the increase of archaeological exploration. These scholars all touched in some way the opinion that the supernatural views of Christianity were adopted from elsewhere, and that the supernatural views were not only broader than Christianity but also older, and had earlier made their way into marginal versions of Judaism.

In all this speculation there was nothing inherently unlikely, but the theses were, and are, unprovable. On the other hand, the case for accepting that there was a Jesus of history can rest on the modest lines of a Schmiedel; that is to say, do passages in the New Testament make more sense by assuming that there was a Jesus than by denying it? The Gospel speaks of the sisters and brothers of Jesus; in the early Church the view arose that Mary was perpetually virgin, and to this day a usual Roman Catholic interpretation is that these sisters and brothers were cousins. If Jesus had no sisters and brothers, why should the Church, ascribing perpetual virginity to Mary, have invented them? Why invent a Jesus who preached the early end of the world? Why invent some obscure Jew, from that obscure region of Palestine, Galilee? The best refutation of the "Christ Myth" school came from an English scholar, F. C. Conybeare, who had himself reached a skeptical position about Christian dogma; as a consequence, his defense of the proposition that Jesus was a historical character was in no sense special pleading, but an able, balanced inquiry into the evidence and the probabilities.[26]

9.

In the same period in which these denials were being written with so much zeal, a British Jew, Claude G. Montefiore, published an extensive series of books, three titles of which are of especial interest in the present context. The first of these is the clue to the other two; it is his two-volume *The Synoptic Gospels*, first published in 1909, with a second edition in 1927. This commentary on the Gospels has a number of characteristics. As to its breadth, Montefiore quoted from many Christian commentators of the time. As a consequence, a student wishing to get a good summary of Gospel scholarship in the early 1900's can quite possibly get this better from Montefiore than anywhere else. As to disposition, Montefiore shared with British New Testament scholars a shunning of that radicalism which characterized the Germans, with the result that one working through Montefiore emerges with an impression of much more reliability in the Gospels than one gets from Schweitzer's totally different but somewhat overlapping work. As to point of departure, Montefiore was a liberal, a leader in the Reform movement in British Jewry. He was without the restraints that many a more traditional Jew might have felt, and, as would be natural, he felt as free to evaluate Christendom as he did Judaism. While Montefiore always made it clear that he wrote from the bias of liberal Judaism, his works are as near an approach to objective scholarship as can be envisioned. In tone, Montefiore was a master stylist, who wrote with great lucidity. He also wrote with a unique combination of forthrightness and gentleness, and while he had no reluctance at expressing judgments adverse to Christianity, he expressed them with such palpable honesty and good will as to have been devoid of offensiveness. This disinclination to offend Christianity offended some fellow Jews, as we shall see, for there have been Jews, understandably, who regard any criticism of Christianity which is not strident as the equivalent of capitulation.

The second book was *Rabbinic Literature and Gospel Teachings,* published in 1930. In this book Montefiore selected a large number of passages which seemed to him to have some clear connection, sometimes affirmative though sometimes negative, with rabbinic passages, and he discussed these both as to their meaning and also as to their value. Disclaiming the possession of technical rabbinic scholarship, he enlisted the services of a fine traditional scholar, Herbert Loewe, and he periodically quoted from the comments which Loewe wrote when Montefiore showed him the draft of some section. The proximity of the Pharisees and Jesus is a recurring conviction in Montefiore; he wrote many other books relating to Christianity and the New Testament, and countless essays and book reviews.

The third book, a small one, was *What a Jew Thinks About Jesus*, published in 1935. In Montefiore's view, not only was the Jesus of history not beyond recovery, but Montefiore had a rather clear portrait of him, a high assessment of him, and a very deep admiration of him. He attributed to him not so much originality in his teaching as a certain intensity, a certain emphasis of a prophetic quality on aspects of Judaism at the expense of other aspects, and his difference from Jewish teachings was in this area of emphasis and of intensity. He held Mark to be more historical than Matthew, and Matthew to be more akin to the Talmudic literature than Mark. He was critical of Jewish scholars who entered the field because, as he charged (correctly), their work was fractional, atomistic; he tried to make his own work thorough and all-encompassing. To Montefiore Jesus was a Jew, not a Christian, and Montefiore was very eloquent in his high evaluation of Jesus.

Montefiore represents eclectic scholarship at its best. Perceptive as he was, I recall no single theory of his which was original. Indeed, his almost conscious wish to take a middle position between German radicalism and British conservatism was combined with such personality traits, as those who knew him have told me, as would rule out originality.

Forthright as he was, he never let considerations of style disappear, so that even when he felt that he must protest against the caricaturing of Judaism in the scholarly writings, he did so with clarity, but also with urbanity. He refuted a good many ugly things said about Judaism without once, so far as I know, himself resorting to ugliness. I admire his scholarship greatly, though his conservatism is not to my taste, and though his knowledge of the Jesus of history exceeded what I myself think is valid. I have often not cared too much for his tendency to compare and contrast this or that element in Christianity and Judaism, though I see clearly that, where he admired a Christian matter more than a Jewish, this is in no way in conflict with his unflagging Jewish loyalty. He was a noble scholar and a fine human being, and he was, above all, to those who knew him a gentle, kindly man.

I find it a little shocking to read Asher Ginzberg's attack on Montefiore. Ginzberg was a Zionist who took the pen name Ahad

Ha'am. He was born in the Ukraine in 1856 and died in Tel Aviv in 1927. The backgrounds of the two men could scarcely have been more different. Montefiore was anti-Zionist, as were most Reform leaders in the early twentieth century. Ahad Ha'am interpreted Zionism to be a "spiritual nationalism," of more vivid concern than the religion professed openly by a Montefiore. He wrote a ferocious onslaught on Montefiore. His stature is not enhanced by his obscurantist fury against a very gentle person. Ginzberg called his essay, if we translate the title from Hebrew into English, "On Two Thresholds." To Ahad Ha'am, the wish by Montefiore to understand Christianity was equivalent to the prelude to conversion. It was quite a concession on his part to ascribe to Montefiore even a partial relationship to Judaism.

Joseph Klausner was a native of Wilna in Lithuania, born in 1874. A Zionist, he was a disciple of Ahad Ha'am, and he also moved ultimately to the Holy Land, where he died in 1960. In 1922 he wrote in the revived Hebrew language a book with the title *Jesus of Nazareth*. Translated into a variety of languages, Klausner's book is by far the best known book by a Jew on Jesus. The English translation runs to 413 pages; only at page 229 does Klausner get to Jesus himself. The preliminaries are occupied with a discussion of the sources (pp. 17–128), and then a discussion of the political, economic, and religious backgrounds (pp. 129–228). The last two chapters have the respective titles, "The Character of Jesus and the Secret of His Influence," and "Conclusion: What Is Jesus to the Jews?" As to the former, Klausner attributed to him, first, a complex personality; Jesus was both humble and tolerant, but on the other hand he possessed a belief in his mission which verged on self-veneration. In his teaching he was a Pharisaic rabbi, but concerned with the *haggada* [27] rather than the *halacha;* however, he invested himself with authority and unlike the Pharisees depended but little on Scripture. As to the latter chapter, Klausner, asserting that while Wellhausen was right in stating that Jesus was a Jew, not a Christian, proceeded to comment that though Jesus was not a Christian, he became one, for his history and his teaching severed him from Judaism.

Moreover (and remember that Klausner was a Zionist), he introduced the question of the meaning of Jesus "from the national Hebrew standpoint." Jesus from this standpoint cannot be God, or the Son of God; he cannot be the Messiah, for the kingdom of heaven is not yet come. Nor can Jesus be a prophet, for he lacked political perception and the spirit of "national consolation in the political national sense." He cannot be regarded as a Pharisaic rabbi, for he did not apprehend the positive side in their work nor exert himself as they did to strengthen the national existence.

On the other hand, Jesus is, for "the Jewish nation"—so Klausner went on—a great teacher of morality and an artist in parable. The book ends: "If ever the day should come and [his] ethical code be stripped of its wrappings of miracles and mysticism, the Book of the Ethics of Jesus will be one of the choicest treasures in the literature of Israel for all time."

Klausner did not possess Montefiore's literary skill, nor would he, I suppose, have ever preferred understatement to combative utterance. Christians have told me that they find his book arrogant and condescending, and it is not hard to see why they think this. The section on the political and religious backgrounds has been roundly criticized by rabbinic specialists, and one needs to attribute that section more to imagination than to supporting documents.

His approach to the Gospels exhibits a unique capacity to have reviewed much of the Gospel scholarship and to have remained immune from reflecting it; Klausner was the amateur Talmudist and amateur psychologist applying dilettantism rather whimsically to the Gospel passages.[28] These comments are directed, of course, to Klausner's scholarship on the Gospels, and not to his being Jewish. Yet there is the curious situation relating to Jesus, that Christians are often inordinately eager to cite some Jewish opinion in support of a Christian contention—my own writings have inadvertently served this purpose to some limited extent—with the result that Klausner is often cited by Christians who attribute to him an authority that with all deference he does not deserve. Conservatives especially have taken him to represent not only the Jewish mind but also the epitome of rabbinic learning, apparently unaware of how severely rabbinists have taken him to task. Fundamentalist Christians have especially quoted his *From Jesus to Paul*, for to quote Klausner in this regard can lead to ignoring the acute problems in the Acts of the Apostles.

Klausner's index has only one entry for Montefiore. He said of Montefiore that the latter "attempts to show . . . that the Gospels are generally superior to the Talmud and are Hebrew works which should be acceptable to Jews." This is a completely twisted summary of Montefiore, and it represents spleen rather than acquaintance. Certainly Klausner's bad book would have been inordinately improved by his having drawn on Montefiore's vastly greater scholarship. Klausner proceeded to allude to Ahad Ha'am's essays, approving of the strictures there against Montefiore. One could suppose that it never occurred to Klausner that he himself represented a viewpoint remote from that of traditional Judaism, and that he could himself undergo a comparable treatment from a source more traditional than he. Klausner in fact is dealt with learnedly by a well-known scholar, Armand Kaminka, in an essay in the Hebrew periodical *Ha-Toren* (August 1922, pp. 59–77). In the first part of his essay on Klausner's book Kaminka dealt with scholarly deficiencies in Klausner's work, but the main objection which Kaminka made was that Klausner was guilty of truckling to Christians. He expressed great indignation at Klausner's representing Jesus as a Pharisaic rabbi.[29] Yet Klausner's book has unquestionably affected more Jews than any other Jewish writing on Jesus, for his undoubted Jewish loyalties have seemed to pave the way for additional Jews to feel spiritually prepared to enter into phases of New Testament scholarship.

10.

In the period between Montefiore's book on the Synoptic Gospels and Klausner's book on Jesus there were two significant developments in Christian scholarship. One of these had to do with the Gospels. From the turn of the century until World War I scholars were preoccupied with refining the "two source" hypothesis. The difficulty with the hypothesis was that while it answered many of the questions, it fell short of all of them; various modifications were proposed, chief of which was expanding the two sources into four. The necessity for the latter was the clear evidence that Matthew has material absent from Mark and Luke, and Luke has material absent from Mark and Matthew. The "four source" hypothesis stated that Matthew and Luke each had some special source from which they drew their data.[30] But insofar as there remained a deep interest in the historic Jesus, the deficiency in the study of the Gospel sources was that the issue of historical credibility was not solved, for a source might well be as unhistorical as a Gospel which used the source.

The conclusion of scholars had been that the Gospels represented the faith of the developing Church, rather than of Jesus himself. Was there some way, some objective way, in which one might discern the difference between an item authentically connected with Jesus and an item produced by the Church? The answer which arose was derived from Old Testament study. It took its point of departure from the question, how did some particular item work its way into the putative source? In 1919, a German scholar, K. L. Schmidt, wrote a book, *Der Rahmen der Geschichte Jesu* ("The Framework of the History of Jesus"), which made the observation, especially respecting Mark, that the connective material binding incident to incident was extremely vague both as to time and place. Out of this observation there arose the conclusion that a source, or even a Gospel, resulted from the weaving together of items which antecedently had been quite separate, especially such items as had been utilized in Christian teaching and preaching. Such an individual item is known by the term *pericope*, a generic term to include an episode, an incident, or merely a teaching.

Next, there occurred to two German scholars the idea of studying the individual pericopes not simply in their context in the Gospels, but rather from the standpoint of what changes the item had passed through from its inception until its inclusion in a Gospel. Both of the scholars felt that the questions could be answered by noting the course of the change of materials in all folklores, for, so it was held, the "rules" of folklore are everywhere pretty much the same. The external form of a pericope might well be a clue to its relative antiquity, for the rules of folklore would suppose that an item passed from simplicity to complexity; thus some mere statement by Jesus could, in the course of transmission of oral folk material, be converted into a narrative episode to which his statement was either the conclusion, or else, reversing things, the shaping factor. Since this study concentrated on the *external form* of the pericopes, it was known in German as *Form Geschichte* ("form history"); it became conventional, though, to refer to it in English as form *criticism*. The two scholars and their works were Martin Dibelius, *Die Formgeschichte des Evangeliums* ("The Form History of the Gospels"), published in 1919; and Rudolf Bultmann, *Die Geschichte der synoptischen Tradition* ("The History of the Synoptic Tradition"), published in 1921.[31] Each began his study by first classifying the materials under categories to indicate the forms: a saying, an episode, an extended episode, and the like. Dibelius was much more conservative than Bultmann. The latter, while he peeled off the layers of growing tradition ostensibly to restore the original material to what it was in Jesus' time, or indeed from Jesus' lips, turned out to attribute virtually everything to the Church, finding nothing to attribute to Jesus except the eschatology.[32] From Schweitzer's time to the end of World War I there had been reborn a kind of conservative liberalism in Gospel scholarship, a development to be discussed below; as a result, Bultmann in particular was severely attacked for what an American reviewer called his excessive skepticism.[33] Form criticism dominated Gospel scholarship through World War II.

The second development alluded to above involved a change that took place in a general attitude toward Scripture. The trend which we have been tracing so far was, as we have emphasized, strongly centered in history, and its results were pre-eminently negative. To the nineteenth-century liberal, this negative character was not too greatly disturbing, for it seemed possible, notwithstanding, to the liberals that they could rescue some residual bits and pieces of history and fashion some theological approach either from them or without regard to them. Moreover, the fashioning of the liberal mentality owed a great debt to eighteenth- and nineteenth-century optimism, which believed that man was making progress and that everything was getting better than it had been. The eighteenth and nineteenth centuries had witnessed the end of tyranny in the Western countries, the growth of political democracy, the cessation of slavery, and the rapid expansion of the industrial system. Though human problems still survived, as in the instance of poverty and the dislocations and deprivations of the working classes, and the debilitating effects of child labor, it was deemed that man surely had the intelligence whereby he could solve all these problems. Indeed, there had arisen along with the evident need for social reform the theory that just and equitable social reform necessitated that the problems be viewed in the light of Christian ethics. In Europe various political parties arose with names such as the "Christian Democratic" party. Naturally, the authority of Jesus was sought as a sanction for the proposed reforms, and the theory arose that Jesus had been primarily a social reformer. A movement known as the "Social Gospel" emerged to emphasize the role of Christians in reform movements. I confess to being a great admirer of the purposes and achievements of the Social Gospel.

It could be argued, and it was, that the interpretation of Christianity as social reform magnified ethics at the expense of faith. Certainly the case could be made, as it was, that there was little essential difference between the proposals for Christian and secular reform, so that one could legitimately wonder about the *religious* aspect of the Christian reform proposals. Since it was out of the liberal scholarship that Jesus as a social reformer had emerged, liberalism and social reform were naturally regarded as intertwined (though even liberal scholars could reject social reform, as some did, Harnack for example). The theological undergirding of the social reforms was, if I may say so, rather skimpy, and highly selective. Moreover, the implication in Christian reform was that man, not God, was the agent through whom reforms were to be achieved. There is a strong motif in Christianity, which runs from Paul through Augustine and to Calvin, which attributes to man a powerlessness to achieve alone; indeed, in Christian thought the theme is found repeatedly that only God can work man's salvation. There is a somewhat similar theme in Judaism stressing man's human limitations, but it has the distinctive difference of not negating nearly so completely man's capacity to achieve, and also of expecting from God, as it were, not the achievement, but the guidance and inspiration to man to enable man to achieve.

To some Christians who re-examined their position in the light of the great tragedy of World War I, the opinion that man was capable of progress seemed eternally refuted, and to such Christians an ethic heightened at the expense of discarding so much of traditional theology seemed both distorted and superficial. Thus, in the context of reassessment by Christians of liberalism, and their properly finding things to criticize, there arose the beginnings of a return to orthodoxy, but on a new basis and not the traditional one. It sought to reinstate doctrines that liberals had abandoned, such as the virgin birth, literal resurrection, and man's inability to progress on his own initiative and abilities; it reinstated these by regarding them as intuitively or subjectively acceptable, that is, "existentially valid."

The reassessment of Christian doctrine applied itself also to biblical scholarship. Since the results of the liberal scholarship were so pointedly negative, it was clear that historical scholarship had only one destiny, complete frustration in the firm establishment of any large substance in the Gospels as unquestionably historical. A new mode of scholarship was needed, one which would find some substitute for the liberal emphasis on historical matters, one which would go beyond mere historical study and the seeming need for historical proof, and concern itself with the spiritual meaning of Scripture. While the initial devotees of "neo-orthodoxy" were recruited from the field of theology and not from biblical scholarship, the influence began to spread from the one to the other, and toward the end of the 1920's the inroads made into biblical scholarship foreshadowed the likelihood of the continued growth of neo-orthodoxy and the decline of liberalism.

To one who stands outside Christianity, there seems little reason to question the aptness of the neo-orthodox criticism of liberalism. Certainly liberalism was marred by exactly those blemishes ascribed to it, especially a view that man had full capacity to work out his destiny unaided, and, in the field of Bible, an excessive preoccupation with questions of historical data rather than with theological doctrine that individuals could apply to their own lives.

For example, liberal scholars asked if Jesus was indeed tempted by the devil; the neo-orthodox scholar asked what is the meaning to the modern reader of the story of the temptation. Neo-orthodoxy as a method could at the same time deny a historical incident and yet find meaning for the student in what he interpreted the passage to connote. That is, the neo-orthodox person reinstated the validity of traditional Gospel doctrine by reclaiming what he believed to be its spiritual implication, even while he, with the liberals, could deny, if need be, the historical basis.

Neo-orthodoxy could, and did, raise questions at least as profound as those raised by liberalism, for liberalism had arisen because orthodoxy seemed inadequate. But it did not in any sense follow that the subsequent inadequacy of liberalism in itself proved the automatic adequacy of neo-orthodoxy. The newness in the bases of *neo*-orthodoxy was not discernible in learning or logic but, as we have said, only in the subjectivity of its assertions. As a consequence, there was needed some buttressing philosophical approach, and this in part lay at hand and was soon to be developed into religious existentialism. It must here suffice to indicate that the old-fashioned liberal asked about a passage, what is its precise meaning? The existentialist would phrase the question, what does the passage mean to me? Obviously, existentialism could run the risk of imputing a merely subjective outlandish meaning to a given passage; hence, biblical scholarship appeared still to be needed in order to create certain controls. But clearly the historically oriented scholarship was to serve, for those who still wanted it at all, as merely the prelude to existential treatment. There began to develop, too, a new kind of "biblical theology." The old biblical theology had been mostly

JESUS THE MAN 99

a classification of the ideas found in Scripture; the new was the assertion of the necessary total relevancy of all of Scripture.

Since the New Testament literature contains so many passages which are anti-Jewish, there could be, at least in theory, this difference between the liberal and the neo-orthodox, that the liberal could feel that the anti-Jewish passages reflected an age of controversy and are intelligible against such a background, and that a modern Christian is free to reject anti-Jewish sentiments. The neo-orthodox insistence, however, on the continuing relevancy of all of the New Testament implied that the anti-Jewish sentiments could also be of abiding value.[34] Neo-orthodoxy might well have taken its turn to dismay Jews. That it did not do so may be the result of a book of considerable importance, this by a liberal, George Foot Moore.

No finer representative of old-fashioned liberalism and its direct intellectual honesty is to be found, in areas of interest to Jews, than the writings of this American Presbyterian of Harvard University. In 1921 Moore wrote an essay in the *Harvard Theological Review* called "Christian Writers on Judaism." He gave a rather full survey of what Christians in various ages had written about Jews. In the last part of his essay he dwelt on the scholarship in Germany at the end of the nineteenth century, that scholarship which had found the Jesus of history at variance with the Judaism of his day, and which had discerned in Judaism the "dry, arid, and sterile" legalism which I have described above. Moore noted, in the first place, that a Jesus at variance with Judaism reversed the trend of all previous Christian writings, for always before, except in early heretical circles, the assertion had been of a Jesus at home in Judaism and of a Christianity which was continuous with it. In the second place, Moore questioned the validity of a description of Judaism which emerged not from a total study of Judaism inquired into on its own terms, but from one which limited itself to those restricted items where Christianity and Judaism touched each other. Judaism is distorted, for example, when there is attributed to it the same measure of attention to the Messiah which is given the Messiah in Christianity. Moore expressed himself quite sharply about Christian writers whose knowledge of the ancient rabbinic literature was derived from anthologies in Latin, or whose knowledge was so small that they eschewed even these anthologies, and constructed their view of Judaism, instead, from Apocrypha and Pseudepigrapha—literature, which it will be recalled, Jews did not preserve. In the third place, Moore made specific inquiry into the writings and the competency of three German scholars (Schuerer, Weber, and Bousset) [35] whose works seemed to have become authoritative for lesser scholars, and Moore minced no words in documenting the deficiencies of these three. In 1927 Moore published his two-volume *Judaism in the First Centuries of the Christian Era: The Age of the Tannaim.* (Later he added a third volume of notes.) His book is one which, negatively, no Jew has had occasion to find serious fault with, and which, affirmatively, is usually regarded even by traditional Jews as a work of rare grace and impeccable scholarship.

Moore is not the only Christian writer in the past half-century who has tried to write accurately about Jews and Judaism. Travers Herford wrote a small book, *The Pharisees,* in 1913; a second, enlarged edition was published in 1924. In it, Herford defended the Pharisees, who are attacked bitterly in the New Testament. Two Germans, Paul Billerbeck, who did most of the work, and Hermann Strack, whose name appears first on the title page, published an immense work, *Kommentar zum Neuen Testament aus Talmud und Midrasch,* in 1922; this was in the train of earlier anthologies but differed from them in being in German rather than in Latin, and in having a much greater number of examples. Indeed, the difficulty with the Strack-Billerbeck anthology is that its devotion to completeness led to the inclusion of matters which are sheer irrelevancies. Besides, Strack and Billerbeck had a unique capacity to cite endless passages which show Jesus and the rabbis saying the same thing, but they invariably managed to discover some aspect in which what Jesus says in the context of saying the same is superior to what the rabbis said.[36]

Moore's book serves not only as a corrective to Strack and Billerbeck but in scholarly circles its eminence has been such that it has created a new tone in the Christian assessments of Judaism. I have deliberately checked this by examining various Introductions to the New Testament written before and after Moore's book, and I have noticed in those books written after Moore's (that is, the books by scholars) the absence of the hostile and condescending approach found in those written before. I know of no area where anti-Jewish feeling, both toward Jews and toward Judaism, is now as rare as it is in the domain of Christian Bible scholars.

11.

The tone of Moore from the Christian side and Montefiore from the Jewish reflected and helped to crystallize a mood as a result of which Christian and Jewish scholars were able to communicate with each other in an atmosphere of common search for the truths which scholarship uniquely can discover. The rise of neo-orthodoxy threatened to diminish that communication, and might well have done so, had not Moore written his authoritative book at the time that he did, and had it not been that Hitlerism raised in a new context the issue of anti-Jewish sentiments for Christians. At a number of occasions in the nineteenth century, the disabilities laid on Jews, or the pogroms, as in Damascus in 1840 and in Russia in the 1880's, called forth from important Protestant leaders sturdy condemnations, and stirring words of rapport with Jews. In this background, Hitlerism raised for Christians the question of the possible historic connection between Christian anti-Jewish sentiments and those of the Nazis, and Christians in abundance disavowed Nazi anti-Semitism and accompanied their disavowal with the repudiation of Christian anti-Jewish sentiment and even doctrine. The Swiss theologian Karl Barth presents the paradox that his theological writings have more than one echo of traditional Christianity's attitude toward Judaism, but Barth himself was one of the Christians who openly rejected Hitler's anti-Semitism at great personal cost to himself. A rarity among New Testament scholars was Gerhard Kittel, who became a Nazi. He edited an immense and important dictionary, *Theologisches*

Wörterbuch zum Neuen Testament. This work is now being translated into English. At the meeting of the Society of Biblical Literature held in December 1963, Markus Barth, Karl's son, now an American, delivered an impromptu eloquent warning to his colleagues to beware of anti-Jewish passages in the Kittel dictionary. I could give multiple examples of such nobility. To choose but two, when Edgar J. Goodspeed published his Life of Jesus in 1950, his anti-Jewish passages were vigorously and eloquently denounced by Franklin Young; also, *Ancient Judaism and the New Testament,* by Frederick C. Grant (New York, 1959), is remarkable for the combination of Christian fidelity and the honest and appreciative estimate of Judaism.

I am here saying two things, first, that I can attest to the support of Jews which has come from such neo-orthodox theologians as the eminent Reinhold Niebuhr, whose sympathy has not been surpassed; and, second, that neo-orthodoxy has nevertheless re-erected some of the barriers to communication on basic Jewish-Christian relationships which the age of liberalism had reduced.

The growth of communication between Jews and Christians was inevitable in the freedom of Western countries. There is a sense in which Montefiore and Klausner, however sturdily Jewish they are and however limited their scholarship may appear to be, represent an honest quest to discover the historic role of Jesus the Jew. Where Jews live in some amity with next door neighbors who are Christians, it is inevitable that Jews ask themselves who and what was Jesus, and Christians ask them what their point of view toward Jesus is. However much some Jews have been disturbed by the mere asking of this question, the fact remains that it is a recurrent Jewish and Christian question.

The level on which the question has been asked, or the manner of its asking, has not uniformly pleased Jews. I suppose that in the 1920's no American rabbi was more beloved of the Jewish "masses" than Stephen S. Wise of New York. In January 1925, Wise spoke at his services on Klausner's book and, going beyond Klausner, reclaimed Jesus for Judaism. Within two weeks Wise had undergone a considerable amount of personal abuse, and he felt impelled to resign his presidency of both the American Zionist Organization and the American Jewish Congress.

I have read Wise's address, and I can comment that it had at least this infelicity, it was not a well-informed sermon. Yet the conclusion seems inescapable that the uproar was caused not so much by what Wise had said, but who it was who was saying it, and at what juncture. American and German rabbis had earlier delivered many a sermon on Jesus with a comparable viewpoint, but they had escaped the public notice that Wise's sermon attracted.

A French priest, Joseph Bonsirven,[37] collected the sermons on Jesus, mostly of American rabbis, mostly Reform, and in 1937 published a little book, *Les Juifs et Jésus; attitudes nouvelles;* this book, "The Jews and Jesus; New Attitudes" has not been translated into English. Bonsirven cited the most eminent rabbis of the time, even quoting their words. He expressed himself as pleased that the historic Jewish aversion to Jesus has been replaced by a friendly attitude. He went on to say, however, that what the Jewish writers he cited were doing was reclaiming Jesus for themselves, and he lamented that they were not bringing themselves to Christ.

Bonsirven was exactly right on both counts. There is a quite long tradition among Jews in the West of reclaiming Jesus for Judaism,[38] and I suspect that in some Jewish circles not only is there no questioning of the propriety of reclamation, but it is even an axiom in the form that Jesus was a Jew, and therefore "ours." Before Hitler, one could document a Jewish interest in Jesus which, during and after Hitler, understandably receded.

In the same period, Christian biblical scholarship tended to divert its interest from Jesus the man to an interest in Jesus the Christ. Since I deal here with movements and trends and not with individuals, my point is that whereas one might have thought in the 1900's and 1910's that Jewish and Christian scholars were on the threshold of some incipient common understanding of Jesus, today that common understanding has again become remote. The older Gospel scholarship was easy for Jews to read and understand; today's scholarship has so shifted to the theological as to be very hard to understand and even to read.

It is my opinion that Jews and Christians are farther apart today on the question of Jesus than they have been in the past hundred years, this despite other ways in which Judaism and Christianity have drawn closer to each other than ever before.

12.

Then what has the accumulated scholarship of the past century and a half contributed to our knowledge of Jesus? The answer has to be that the Jewish backgrounds have become better understood, the Graeco-Roman environment, especially the religious quests among pagans, better known, and the relations of the Gospels to each other and to other Christian writings better assessed; also, archaeology has broadened and deepened our knowledge of both late Judaism and early Christianity.

A little attention to the Dead Sea scrolls may be a good prelude to move us on to our conclusions. Like many an archaeological discovery, the Dead Sea scrolls were newsworthy enough to be reported in the general press, but they had the additional attraction that they were, if their date between the years 100 B.C. and A.D. 100 could be accepted, the first and only major discovery of documents from the age of Jesus. Since the public impression had already been that archaeology in some way confirmed Scripture, it was hoped, expected, and prematurely announced that the scrolls were verifying Christian claims. Sometimes this alleged verification took the form of finding in some of the scrolls, through misreading them, or through supplying readings where the texts had gaps, so-called precursors of Christianity. The result has been that materials in the scrolls have been deemed to anticipate similar material in the Gospels and Epistles of Paul. One line of such reasoning has run in the peculiarly perverse way that there was nothing essentially new in Christianity because its main theological contentions were already found in the Dead Sea scrolls. An opposite view has seemed to concede that the scrolls show a connection with the direct source from which the raw materials of Christianity were drawn, but that Christianity developed these raw materials in its own unique ways. These related but conflicting conclusions have rested on the premise that there was some special connection between the community which had created the scrolls and Christianity, a revival, often unconscious, of the view of Heinrich Graetz noted above. The scroll community was identified with the Essenes, and a good many nineteenth-century theories about the Essenic origin of Christianity were revived. Again, John the Baptist was made a member in good standing of the Essene community, and either through John, or even through his own direct membership, Jesus himself was brought into relationship with the Essenes.

Indeed, one scholar, William F. Albright, has used the evidence from the scrolls to repudiate the common opinion of Gospel scholars that the Gospel According to John was the latest Gospel; he believes it to be the earliest, and that what has antecedently seemed to scholars to be Grecian was in reality a product of that type of Palestinian Judaism which the scroll community represents. He goes still further and expresses the judgment that the scrolls have demonstrated that the discourses in John, universally attributed to an age much later than that of Jesus, were quite apt to be Jesus' own words, and that a Jesus who spoke in one way in the Synoptic Gospels did not rule out his speaking in a different way in John, and hence the discourses in John are *ipsissima verba*. In a word, there have been those scholars who hailed the scrolls as confirming the reliability of the Gospel records, this after a century and a half of Gospel scholarship had gone in exactly the opposite direction.

With the progressive study of the scrolls a good many of the initial enthusiastic judgments turned out to be unpersuasive. Even for those willing to date the scrolls between 100 B.C. and A.D. 100, there are two important factors which have attracted more continuing attention. The first of these is that the scrolls contain very little material of that kind which enables them to be dated around specific known events, and lack even more noticeably the names of people. Jesus, Peter, and Paul go unnamed in the scrolls. Hence, the attribution of a relationship between earliest Christianity and the scrolls is a matter of disputed inference, and not a case in which mere citation could clinch the issue. The second factor, consequently, is that the scrolls serve at best as adding illumination to the Jewish background of Christianity. The question, next, is whether the scrolls throw light on the specific background of Christianity, or whether they merely add to the material already available relating to the general background. (Some scholars seem unaware that, even prior to the discovery of the scrolls, illuminating background materials were already at hand.) There appears to me to be as yet no consensus among scholars on this latter issue, for there are those who insist that the scrolls point to the specific background, and others (which is the view that I favor) that their contribution is only general and not specific. I would personally emphasize that the scrolls have contributed in quantity little to what we already had, and that in quality this little is worthy but of much less significance than it was sometimes initially deemed. The scrolls are "important," in my opinion, only in themselves, and not in the light that they shed on Christianity. For the scrolls turn out not to have added one jot to the previous knowledge about Jesus.

We are still dependent for knowledge about Jesus only on New Testament materials, the chief of which are the Gospels. The century and a half of Gospel study can be summarized in this way: Strauss began by denying virtually everything in the Gospels, but without studying the relationship of the Gospels to each other. Renan differed from Strauss in that he was arbitrary in rejecting some materials as legendary and accepting other materials as historical. The testing of the theory of the priority of Mark, by inquiring into the relationships of the Gospels to each other in the interest of discovering an objective way by which to approach the question of reliable history, was an initial step corrective of Strauss's wholesale denial and of Renan's arbitrariness. The "discovery" of Q seemed to provide, in itself and in Mark, two sources which by virtue of their earliness suggested a greater reliability in them than in Matthew and in Luke. But, in turn, the work of Wrede undermined the theory that the early source was more historical, for Wrede's conclusions made Mark as unhistorical as Matthew and Luke. Since neither the "two source" nor the "four source" hypothesis solved the problem of historical reliability, form criticism was resorted to in an effort to recover the materials which went into the early sources and to sift this material in order to isolate the historical form from the unhistorical. While form criticism set forth a way by which historical materials could be recovered, the conclusions of form criticism chanced to be abundantly negative and its method unpersuasive, even to those who were willing to receive the negative results, on the basis of their opinion that form criticism was marred by extreme subjectivity.

By and large the opinion of scholars has been that the Gospels reflect more adequately the piety of the Church than they reflect Jesus himself. Out of this general opinion there has arisen in very recent years what is called the "new quest" for the historical Jesus. These questers believe that it will be possible through continued study to find in the teaching and preaching of the early Church some set of reliable reflections of Jesus, on the premise that his impact on early preachers and teachers was vivid enough to create unmistakable specifics. As yet this type of investigation has been proposed as a method but not carried to the point of conclusions.

There is, then, no unmistakable agreement on the Jesus of history to be found in the labors and written works of New Testament scholars. What Schweitzer said almost sixty years ago is just as true now, that the Jesus of history is beyond recovery, and that the Jesus of Gospel scholars of the nineteenth century, and of the twentieth, never existed, for that Jesus emerges more from the intuition and from the anachronisms of the scholars than from the pages of the Gospels.

II THE MEANING

It would be easy for someone like me to set forth some ingenious statement about Jesus. I have ample Jewish predecessors to rely

on if I were to wish to choose one of the several options. I could
with Graetz term Jesus an Essene, with Geiger term him a Phari-
see, with Montefiore term him a prophet, and with countless
others term him a rabbi (even though rabbi, *as a title,* appears to
be later than the age of Jesus). I am withheld from such a statement by the very nature of the problems which have created the
variety of opinion among the Christians. It is the problem that the
Gospels, the primary sources, are writings from an age at least
four decades or more removed from the time of Jesus, and that
the Gospels so intertwine authentic material about Jesus with the
pious meditation of the Church that I know of no way to separate
the strands and to end up with some secure and quantitatively
adequate body of material. I simply do not know enough about
him to have an opinion, and I surely do not have enough to set
him, as it were, in some one single category.

But beyond this, it is my conviction that the Gospels are not
telling about the man that scholarship seeks, but about the human
career of a divine being. To search the Gospels for the man seems
to me to involve a distortion of what is in the Gospels. New Testament scholarship has not succeeded in isolating the man Jesus,
Jesus the Jew.

Yet, suppose someone were to say, "You keep stressing the
scholars. Aren't you making too much of scholarship? [39] Forget
for a moment the problems of historical reliability. Here are the
Gospels; they tell you about Jesus. Isn't it possible for you to have
some view of him which is the essence of the Gospels but kept
free from the piddling questions of whether this or that detail is
historical?"

Possibly something of this kind is possible, though just how
satisfying it would be is a different matter. I have at various times
tried to formulate some such thing, but I have not succeeded in
satisfying myself. I once spoke, on the spur of the moment, of
likening the portrait of Jesus to an oil painting rather than a
photograph; if one stands too near to an oil painting, he sees the
brush marks rather than the portrait.

It seems to me not to violate the documents or that scholarship
which I have imbibed to think of Jesus as someone who had gifts

of leadership and who was something of a teacher. I believe too that I discern in him a Jewish loyalty at variance with the views both of Christian and Jewish partisans who, through opposing motives that cancel each other out, detach him from Judaism. I believe that Jesus firmly believed that the end of the world was coming soon. I believe that he believed himself to be the Messiah, and that those scholars who deny this are incorrect.

I own to seeing no originality in the teachings of Jesus, for I hold that those passages which deal with his supernatural role reflect not his authentic words but the piety of the developing Church. As to those teachings which are conceivably his, they seem to me to be of a piece with Jewish teaching, and that they range from the commonplaces of that Jewish teaching through a sporadic flash of insight that other Jewish teachers also achieved. Yet I feel that all too often the question of originality is a misguided one, for it can often resolve itself into the unimportant question of mere priority. To my mind the crux of the issue about the Golden Rule is not the question of whether Hillel said it before Jesus, or Jesus before Hillel (Hillel chances to be a little earlier than Jesus), nor whether Hillel's formula in the negative is superior or inferior to Jesus' formula in the affirmative (the "Western Text" of Acts gives the Golden Rule in the negative formula!), nor whether both are, or are not, derived from Leviticus 19. To my mind the issue is that of value, not of priority; I find that there is more in the teachings of Jesus that I admire than that I do not; indeed, purely by chance I would deny that the hateful and hating chapter Matthew 23 goes back authentically to Jesus. There is, then, a general sense in which I see abiding values in many of the teachings of Jesus, and I also see that Christians have found affirmative values in passages which do not stir me; for example, I believe that Christians have been motivated to noble act and deed by the injunction not to resist evil, but I cannot in good conscience agree with this sentiment.

I cannot ascribe to the teachings of Jesus a striking uniqueness in particulars which in honesty I do not discern. The uniqueness of Jesus would lie not in single particulars, but in the combination of facets, in the totality of what we may perhaps glimpse of him, and not in any one isolated way. Thus he was in part a teacher, a Jewish loyalist, a leader of men, with a personality unquestionably striking enough to be a leader, and his career must have been exceedingly singular for his followers to say that he had been resurrected.

He was a martyr to his Jewish patriotism. So many Jews became martyrs at the hands of later Christians that his martyrdom seems to us perhaps too unexceptionable for special notice. We Jews have so suffered, because Christians in ages past made us suffer, that it is difficult for us to acknowledge that Jesus suffered unusually. I believe that he did. There is to my mind both in the Epistles of Paul and in the Gospels the recurrent note that the career of Jesus was one of triumph; I can certainly acknowledge that martyrdom partakes of the overtone of triumph. Yet the dominant note to me of his career is overwhelmingly one of pathos, of sympathy, that a man, with the normal frailties of men, aspired and labored and worked, and yet experienced defeat.

I must hasten to add that I do not see this as exclusive in the instance of Jesus, or even, for I must be honest, the pre-eminent motif in his experience. But I do see it. Perhaps I would see it in even greater clarity if I could leap across the centuries of the Jewish-Christian tragedy, for just as often as I begin to find myself in warm sympathy with Jesus, I find this sympathy obstructed by a feeling that he remains always in some measure alien to me. When I ask myself why this is so, I do not ascribe it to any conscious bias—this may be the case, but I do not think so—but rather because I am inherently unable to see in Jesus that extra attribute which Christians and quasi-Christians see in him. Perhaps the impediment is not so much what my mind and heart may tell me about Jesus, but simply my resistance to what admirable and noble Christians tell me about him. I can agree that he was a great and good man, but not that he exceeded other great and good men in the excellency of human virtues.

I discern no possible religious assessment of Jesus, either by me or by other Jews. I cannot share in the sentiments of Montefiore which seem to me to fly in the face of prudent scholarship, nor in Klausner's distant dream of a reclaimed Jesus.

I must say most plainly that Jesus has no bearing on me in a religious way. I am aware that some Christians declare that they see in Christianity, with its figure of Jesus, a completeness which eludes them in Judaism. I am not sensible of any such incompleteness, for I neither feel nor understand that my Judaism is in any way incomplete. A religion is, after all, a complex of more than just theological viewpoints, for a religion has its own tone and texture which arise from its history, its group experience, its mores and norms, and even its folkways. I confess that there arises in me from time to time, in moods of self-criticism, some occasional feeling about certain inadequacies in Judaism. For example, I could wish that our exalted Jewish intellectual tradition were less remote than it has been from the Western stream of intellectual history; I could wish that our music had developed beyond the modal, and into Jewish counterparts of Bach, Mozart, and Beethoven; I could wish that we had a richer tradition of art. In such areas, then, I confess to recognizing deficiencies, and, in such a sense, incompleteness. But I do not discern any religious incompleteness which the figure of a Jesus would fill in, just as I see no incompleteness which a Mohammed or a Confucius would fill in.

Culturally, however, the situation is quite different. I own to an affinity for Mozart's liturgical music and to Beethoven's; and if to me by chance Bach does not appeal in the same way, then it is my idiosyncrasy and my loss. The figure of Jesus is part of Western culture, and I hold myself in all truth to be a legatee of and a participant in Western culture. In this sense, the figure of Jesus comes into my ken inevitably, just as he comes into the ken of all Western Jews. I cannot value him above the martyr Socrates, but I cannot conceive of myself as unaware of him, or isolated from him. Since I chance to enjoy folk music, whether from the robust voices of Israeli sabras or from the nasal tones of the Tennessee mountaineers, I also enjoy Christian music, especially the medieval English carols. I am eternally grateful to live in a land and in an age in which I am not constrained, through having felt the hostility of Christians, to cut myself off from that place in Western culture which Jesus occupies. Near Jerusalem there is a Byzantine church to which Israelis go in great numbers to hear organ recitals of Bach; they do not cut themselves off from the great music of Western civilization.

I see no valid reason for Jews to insulate themselves from the Jesus of Western culture, any more than they should, or would, from Plato. If it is retorted that in this attitude there is a risk, that it is hard to mark off the Jesus of culture from the Jesus of religion, then my reply is that Jews are going to run this risk, and only renewed Christian persecution, God forbid, will deter them from it. Here and there some Jew will cross over to Christianity. I know that this happens and will continue to happen. I venture to suppose that these crossings arise much more from Western freedom, and freedom to court and woo, than from theological concessions. To my mind there is a greater likelihood of the perpetuation of Jewish loyalties through the understanding by Jews of where they stand religiously in respect to Jesus than in their retaining this as a somewhat forbidden area, even though it enters into our ken and into our lives.

In context, I am saying that since Jesus occupies a position in Western culture, and since Jews in the West are part of Western culture, Jews will inevitably encounter his figure. Jews need not shy away from such cultural encounter. They will not, and they should not, compromise their convictions about the Christ Jesus of the Christian religion. They should know and understand the Jewish religion, certainly as a higher priority to their understanding Christianity. But Jews can be trusted to discern the difference between the Jesus of religion and the Jesus of Western culture.

Notes

1. The books are: Albert Schweitzer, *The Quest of the Historical Jesus* (Eng. trans. 1906 and later); Shirley Jackson Case, *Jesus through the Centuries,* Chicago, 1932; and C. C. McCown, *The Search for the Real Jesus,* New York, 1940. The article is "From Locke to Reitzenstein; the Historical Investigation

of the Origins of Christianity," by Luigi Salvatorelli, *Harvard Theological Review*, XXII, October 1929, pp. 263–367. See also Morton Enslin, "Biblical Criticism and Its Effect on Modern Civilization," *Five Essays on the Bible* (American Council of Learned Societies), 1960, pp. 30–44.

2. See above, pp. 18–20, the brief, indeed over-brief, characterization of the Gospels.

3. His use of the word "myth" differs from most modern use. In general, "legend" supposes that some basic kernel of history has so grown by additions that the basic kernel is obscured. "Myth," on the other hand, lacks the direct kernel of historicity; it is often a narrative depicting an abstract idea, and while the details of the narrative are unhistorical, the abstract idea depicted had some real historical context. Strauss ascribed a nucleus of historical reliability to "historical myths," but none to "pure myths."

4. He said at the beginning of his last chapter (p. 757): "The results of the inquiry which we have now brought to a close have apparently annihilated the greatest and most valuable part of that which the Christian has been wont to believe concerning his Saviour Jesus. . . ."

5. This question of the literary relationship of the first three Gospels to each other is known among scholars as the "Synoptic problem."

6. In his *Church History*, III, 39, 16.

7. A puzzling phrase then ensues here, to the effect that Mark had recorded these things "but not in order."

8. Strauss and Baur are still today of surpassing value in New Testament study, especially Baur. To both must be credited significant achievements in distinguishing John from the other three Gospels.

9. This is a paraphrase; the reference is to *Sämtliche Werke*, XXIX, pp. 45–67. When Luther was later frustrated in his wish to convert the Jews, he wrote about them even more poisonously than had the Roman Catholics whom he criticized.

10. See above, pp. 21–3.

11. Graetz based this on Matthew 19:10–11.

12. For the latter Graetz used a rabbinic phrase, *Am Ha-Arez*. In rabbinic literature the *Am Ha-Arez* goes undefined. It is a phrase borrowed from Scripture and means literally "the people of the land." The rabbinic literature alludes to the *Am Ha-Arez* as incapable of piety. Just whom and what the rabbis meant is quite uncertain, and the condescending passages are fully balanced, and even overbalanced, by a permeating sympathy for the unlearned. More than one scholar, however, has leaped to the conclusion that, since the rabbis denounce the *Am Ha-Arez* and since Jesus fraternized with tax-collectors and sinners, Jesus was an *Am Ha-Arez*. What is wrong with this conclusion is that the rabbinic literature gives too little data for any firm

knowledge of the *Am Ha-Arez,* and moreover, the Gospels are too complex to justify so simple a summary statement.

13. Such was the case of the Old Testament scholar Julius Wellhausen, who turned his attention to the Gospels late in his life, and who began his book, *Einleitung in die drei ersten Evangelien* (1905), with these words, "Jesus was a Jew, not a Christian."

14. I mention him above, pp. 38–41, in connection with the *Logos,* and in relationship to the alterations in Messianic thought.

15. Because the Church fathers who quoted Josephus extensively did not quote this passage, and because the passage bears clear marks of a Christian viewpoint, most modern scholars regard the entire passage as an interpolation into the text. Only a small handful regard it as by Josephus. There are scholars, though, who believe that the passage was rewritten from its pristine form, some because they do not wish to believe that Jesus would go unmentioned in Josephus, but others from a totally opposite point of departure, because the paragraph is followed by this story: A man, Mundus, wanted to sleep with a virtuous woman named Paulina. Some priests of Isis were bribed to tell Paulina that the god Anubis had fallen in love with her and wanted her to come to him. At the temple in the night, Mundus had his way with Paulina, who reported to her husband that the god had appeared to her. The next incident in Josephus concerns a Roman woman, Fulvia, a convert to Judaism, who entrusted to four deceivers a large gift for the temple in Jerusalem, but these men embezzled the money. Fulvia's husband related the misdeed to the Emperor, Tiberius, who punished the four miscreants by expelling all the Jews from Rome. Such scholars hold that the present passage about Jesus replaces a paragraph about a deception of Mary, this as the first of three about deceived women. This supposed original account was a cynical commentary on the virgin birth, according to these scholars. Such is the interpretation found in *Paulus, Kommentar über das Neue Testament,* I, pp. 140ff., 1800. Strauss quoted it (Eng. trans. p. 139); I encounter it from time to time.

16. This tendency, which is at most inchoate and unsystematic in Renan's work, reappeared significantly in later Christian scholarship.

17. Two American rabbis, Isaac Mayer Wise and Hyman G. Enelow, wrote about Jesus as if Jesus were a nineteenth-century American rabbi.

18. A parable is a brief anecdote which illustrates some point. The marriage guests who became uninvited because they were not ready illustrate the virtue of preparedness. But when the bare parable grows to the point that the host is God, the guests are the Jews, the summoning servants are the prophets, then the parable has become "allegorized." Jülicher, one of the principal scholars in this effort, attempted to pare off the allegorization and thereby arrive at the original parable.

19. Jews call the legal sections *halacha* and the edifying sections *haggada.*

20. "Parallelomania," in *Journal of Biblical Literature*, March 1962.

21. See "Pharisees," *Interpreter's Bible Dictionary*, Vol. III, pp. 774–81.

22. My allegation here is a general one. Significant Christian scholars, especially the more eminent ones of recent decades, have been scrupulously fair, and informed, in assessing rabbinic Judaism. See pp. 99–101.

23. Loisy's view both implies and also clearly states that the Gospels are replete with nonhistorical elements. Tragically, this defense by Loisy of the Church brought about his defrocking and his excommunication by the Church which he defended.

24. It should be noted that there are responsible scholars who understand this verse as in essential harmony with thoroughgoing eschatology.

25. The reader must understand that the author must necessarily generalize. A volume which I applaud, for its scholarship, its honesty, and its manifestly heart-felt abhorrence of anti-Semitism in all its forms, is Morton S. Enslin's *The Prophet from Nazareth*, New York, 1962. Mr. Enslin espouses a thoroughgoing eschatology in which he states that Jesus was mistaken. One might say of his book that it portrays a Jewish Jesus with fullest sympathy for Judaism and unreserved love and reverence for Jesus.

26. Conybeare was capable of writing with acid. His survey of the New Testament, *Myth, Magic, and Morals,* is as anti-Christian as anything I have ever read. His *The Historical Christ* is a skillful denunciation of Robertson and Drews. An excellent later book is by the Frenchman, Maurice Goguel, the translation of which was published under the title *Jesus the Nazarene, Myth or History*, New York, 1926. Goguel was superb in assessing the deniers; his affirmative case, however, was a triumph of piety over scholarship.

27. To repeat, the *haggada* is the edifying aspect of rabbinic literature, the *halacha* the legal aspect.

28. He denied, on a psychological basis, that Jesus could have said, "Father forgive them for they know not what they do." He abstained from noting what is found in every Gospel commentary, that this verse is not found in some of the best ancient manuscripts of the New Testament.

29. Kaminka apologized for his vehemence, especially if his essay should reach Christian eyes, for he said a modern Jew cannot use any of the utterances of Jesus until the pagan cruelties and arrogant assumption of superiority are wiped out. Yet even then, any page of a medieval ethical work would be more precious than this whole alien heritage, of which Kaminka felt no need whatsoever. English readers can find a résumé of Kaminka's essay in *Harvard Theological Review*, XVI, 1923, pp. 93–103. G. F. Moore there added the comment: "Kaminka's criticisms are frequently sound; and if the polemic is bitter and sometimes descends to invective, we may be reminded that the Jews have small reason to admire Christian ethics in application, whether ecclesiastical, political, social, or individual; and, judging the tree by the fruit

it has borne in eighteen centuries of persecution, they not unnaturally resent Christian assertions of its pre-eminence, and still more even the qualified admission of such claims by a Jew." This vein of Christian self-criticism by Moore was destined to find many Christian echoes in the Hitler era, and while it was exceptional when it was written, it has come to be the precursor for a by now frequent Christian attitude, as we shall see.

30. The principal name associated with the "four source" hypothesis is B. H. Streeter, *The Four Gospels*. This book was published in 1924; the intimations of the "four source" hypothesis appeared earlier.

31. Klausner made no mention of Schmidt, Dibelius, or Bultmann. Dibelius's book was translated into English under the title *From Tradition to Gospel*. Bultmann's book has been translated only very recently.

32. Form criticism reached its conclusions through asking, what is the "real-life situation" of this pericope? The original phrase, *Sitz im Leben*, became the slogan of devotees of this type of study.

33. Bultmann published *Jesus: the Word* in 1926; it was translated in 1934. It has little connection with Bultmann's scholarly writing, in which Jesus is virtually unknown; Bultmann now found him known to the extent of calling men to basic decisions and preaching a radical ("root") obedience to God, transcending the Jewish view of obedience.

34. A Christian, A. Roy Eckardt, wrote his *Christianity and the Children of Israel* (New York, 1948), on precisely this facet of neo-orthodoxy, for Eckardt, as his book reveals, was profoundly disturbed at the implication that anti-Jewish feeling should be regarded as essential to Christianity. His thoughtful book merits continuing interest.

35. Emil Schuerer's book, translated into English under the title *A History of the Jewish People in the Time of Jesus Christ*, 2 volumes (Volume I encompasses two books and Volume II three), Edinburgh, 1872. The particular chapter Moore addressed himself to is "Life under the Law," found in II, ii, pp. 90–125. The other two works have not been translated. They are: Wilhelm Bousset, *Die Religion des Judentums im neutestamentlichen Zeitalter*, Berlin, 1903 (a second edition, Tübingen, 1926, substitutes *späthellenistischen* for *neutestamentlichen*); and Ferdinand Weber, *System der altsynagogalen palästinensischen Theologie*, Leipzig, 1880.

36. I treated Strack and Billerbeck at some length in "Parallelomania," *Journal of Biblical Literature*, March 1962. I did not comment there on a book in German by Paul Fiebig, *Die Gleichnisrede Jesu im Lichte der rabbinischen Gleichnisse des neutestamentlichen Zeitalters*, Tübingen, 1912, which, discussing the parables of Jesus and the rabbis, made the point that the parables of Jesus were drawn from nature, while those of the rabbis were not. A Jew, Asher Feldman, replied by publishing his *The Parables and Similes of the Rabbis; Agricultural and Pastoral*, Cambridge, 1924.

37. An earnest student of rabbinic literature, Bonsirven published in 1934–35 his *Le Judaisme palestinien au temps de Jésus-Christ,* which has been abridged and published in English under the title *Palestinian Judaism in the Time of Jesus Christ,* New York, 1964. A comparison of Bonsirven's book with that of Moore is instructive. Moore's method was to provide the facts and let the interpretation flow from them; Bonsirven's book is not so much a description of rabbinic Judaism as a partisan assessment of it.

38. See my "Isaac Mayer Wise's Jesus Himself," in *Essays in American Jewish History.*

39. An opinion which one finds sporadically among Jews is that of John Cournos, in *An Open Letter to Jews and Christians,* New York, 1938, p. 12: "Jesus was not only a Jew. He was the apex and the acme of Jewish teaching . . ." This human Jesus of Cournos is as remote from Christian convictions as he is from the contents of the New Testament and of rabbinic literature. Cournos proceeded to cite Joseph Jacobs, *As Others Saw Him,* New York, 1925, and its introduction by Harry A. Wolfson, "How the Jews Will Reclaim Jesus," but he seriously distorted both (pp. 176–9), in pursuing his counsel to Jews to reclaim Jesus. He proposed (p. 180) that Zionists reclaim him in conformity with what he describes as the "admirable Socialist programme in Palestine" (p. 182).

It is this sort of thing which by its unrestrained elasticity persuades me to remain within the rigid confines of scholarly, pedantic knowledge.

Perhaps the opinion of Martin Buber, *Pointing the Way* (Eng. trans.), New York, 1957, p. 18, might be referred to here, though it is quite different from that of Cournos. Buber wrote that he believed firmly that the Jewish community would some day recognize Jesus as part of the context of a Messianic development occurring over millennia, but never as the Messiah who has come, for, Buber went on to say, redemption has not yet occurred. (I have wondered whether Christians regard Buber's opinion as praise, or as faint praise.) A lack of academic substance in Buber's view on Jesus is illustrated in another reference, this time to *Hasidism,* New York, p. 114, where he described Jesus as one who erroneously claimed messiahship, and who differed from the subsequent and equally mistaken claimants in that Jesus was the purest and most legitimate of all, and the one most endowed with real Messianic power. The pedant can hardly take Buber too seriously, for he must wonder, for example, just how the Messianic endowments of Messiahs, authentic or mistaken, can be weighed. The Yiddish novelist, Scholem Asch, wrote a series of novels on Jesus (*The Nazarene*) and Paul. To my mind these books are tedious, and I should warn the unwary that the Judaism which Asch attributes to the age of Jesus is in reality that of pre-modern Poland. Antagonistic as I am to Asch's works, when I read the merciless attacks on him in Chaim Lieberman, *The Christianity of Scholem Asch,* I ended up with a deep sympathy for him.

CHAPTER 5 · The Jewish Reader and
the Gospels

In many an American university a course is taught with some
such title as "The Bible as Literature." Sometimes such a course
enables a state university to include Bible in its curriculum without trespassing into the controversies over the separation of
Church and state; sometimes it is a "nondenominational" way of
letting students become acquainted with the content of Scripture
while avoiding the difficulties inherent in the divergencies of
Christian-Jewish approaches, Catholic-Protestant approaches, and
Modernist-Fundamentalist approaches. The justification for such
courses is that it is preferable for a student to know the content of
Scripture than for him to be ignorant of it.

A supposition in many such courses is that literary qualities,
often of tremendously high attainment, inhere in biblical writing,
and that these qualities can be described. For example, one can
point to the matchless poetry of the Psalms, the beauty and profundity of Job, and the narrative skill in books such as Genesis
and Ruth.

THE JEWISH READER AND THE GOSPELS 119

What this can amount to, often unconsciously, is the subjection of Scripture to a type of literary criticism, with the critic standing, as it were, above the literature and judging it. In such judgments, as in all literary criticism, the would-be critic speaks from some explicit or tacit assumptions about what is good literature and what is bad, and his own personal taste inevitably enters in.

To us Jews, the Gospels are not sacred. When we read them (if we do), we read them as literature, not as Scripture. We inescapably respond, or fail to respond, to them in a way comparable to our responding, or not, to other literature. So frequently are the passages, especially in connection with the death of Jesus, anti-Jewish, that it can be very difficult for us Jews merely to read them.

The challenge to a serious Jewish student of early Christianity is even more acute than that of a general Jewish reader. A serious student cannot overlook, cannot ignore, the historical and religious problems which inhere in the literature, and the merely appreciative is more than difficult to arrive at, in fact, it is impossible.

For someone like me, the Gospels, on the one hand, so recreate the Jewish scene that the recreation must be the result of knowledge and reflection of it, and it cannot be regarded merely as fictional. On the other hand, there is scarcely an item in the Gospels which does not bristle with problems. Let us take one example, the tradition recorded in the first three Gospels that Jesus was baptized in the Jordan River by John the Baptist (not to be confused with the John who wrote the fourth Gospel). As to Jewish baptism, there is some failure on the part of the available Jewish sources to confirm the use of baptism in such a context, but let us overlook this unimportant detail. Matthew reports that John was unwilling to baptize Jesus, for the implication of baptism in the Christian view was that it procured the remission of sins, and Matthew is expressing through his portrayal of John's reluctance to baptize Jesus his aversion to the implication that Jesus had ever sinned. (An apocryphal Gospel, the Gospel of the Nazarenes, portrays Jesus in elaborate discussion with his mother as to whether or not he should submit to baptism.) Luke glosses over the baptism by John, treating it in a subordinate clause, and proceeds to the matter of the descent of the Holy Spirit on Jesus, a theme found in the first three Gospels; but in Luke the Holy Spirit descends on Jesus in the bodily form of a dove, whereas Matthew and Mark say only that the spirit descended on him *like* a dove, that is, not in bodily form. In all three Gospels the heavens open, and a voice speaks, but the three Gospels fail to report identical words on the part of the heavenly voice.

Suppose, though, that we were to recognize that embellishment has entered into the account of the baptism of Jesus, this fact of embellishment would not necessarily lead one to feel he must deny that Jesus was baptized by John. He could affirm it, if he cared to, as a bare detail. But it turns out that material both in the New Testament and elsewhere disclosed that John led what we might call a rival movement to that of Jesus; such seems the inference from Acts and from passages in the Fourth Gospel. If this were the case, then what weight should we give to John's subservience as expressed in Mark 1:7–8, Matthew 3:11, Luke 3:16, and John 1:27, that after him someone is coming (Jesus) whose shoestrings John is unworthy to bend over and untie; and the passage, Matthew 11:11–14, which seemingly disparages John? From yet another viewpoint, the Jewish Messianic belief carried with it the expectation that Elijah the prophet, who according to tradition ascended to heaven without dying, would return to herald the coming of the Messiah. The Gospels regard John as the forerunner of Jesus the Messiah, and they identify John with Elijah. If the general (though not universal) effect is to view John as the precursor of Jesus, then why was there a separate movement on the part of John's followers? Is it possible, since John was well enough known to be spoken of by Josephus, that the relationship between John and Jesus is an artifice resulting from binding the obscure movement led by Jesus to the better known movement led by John, first through asserting that John was no more than the forerunner of the Messiah, and second by proceeding to make the relationship more direct through portraying Jesus as baptized by John? The implication of sin antecedent to baptism results in Matthew's attributing to Jesus that state-ment that John is right in being unwilling to baptize Jesus but that they should proceed to it, "so as to fulfill all righteousness." That is to say, the narrative which attributed the relationship of John to Jesus as involving baptism turned out to have an impli-cation about Jesus which was distasteful to Matthew; and there may be some profound significance in the absence from the Gos-pel According to John of any mention of Jesus' baptism at the hands of John the Baptist. But going a step further, the Gospel According to Luke informs us that Elizabeth, the mother of John the Baptist, was a relative of Mary, the mother of Jesus; both women were pregnant at the same time. Mary went to call on Elizabeth, and when she entered the room where Elizabeth was, the embryonic John the Baptist within Elizabeth leaped for joy, in deference to the as yet unborn but already conceived Jesus.

That Jesus was baptized by John could accord with what we know about Jewish practice of the time, but can nevertheless raise uncertainties or even doubts. Were we confronted by a sim-ple statement, bare and laconic, that Jesus had been baptized by John, we should have little reason to doubt it. But an embellished account which itself created an inner Christian problem and exists in the broader context of the elusive nature of the historical relationship between John and Jesus alerts us to the possibility that even the baptism of Jesus by John, credible as it might be, is a fiction.[1]

Perhaps now I have managed to make clear the dilemma for the Jewish student. On the one hand, there is a rather good con-gruency between the Jewish materials and the Gospel materials, so as to establish a sense of reliability; on the other hand, each detail in the Gospels seems capable of raising its own set of prob-lems. Was Jesus born in Nazareth or in Bethlehem? Perhaps, as some scholars have suggested, he was actually born in Nazareth, but the ascription of his birth to Bethlehem is the product of proof-texting which suggested that the Messiah must come from Bethlehem. As to his birth in Nazareth, that city's existence fails to be confirmed by any mention before or during Jesus' lifetime; moreover, the word *nazir*, used to describe a person dedicated to

God (as Judges 13:2–5 report of Samson; see also Numbers 6:1–21) has led to the opinion that the passage Matthew 2:23 means not that Jesus was really from Nazareth but only that he was a Nazir.

Similarly, that Jesus entered Jerusalem need raise no doubts, but that he entered in on a borrowed animal, or on two animals in accordance with Matthew's misunderstanding[2] of Zechariah, is quite another problem. Certain details of the unfolding events of the last week can raise the question of whether Old Testament passages suggest incidents which the Gospels create, or rather whether the incidents occurred and thus brought the Old Testament passages to mind. Did Jesus on the cross say, "My God, my God, why have you forsaken me?" Was this an actual, despairing word that he spoke? Or, since it is a quotation from Psalm 22:1, did the Gospel writer, in ignorance of what, if anything, Jesus said, select this heart-rending verse as appropriate to the occasion? Indeed, one can approach the trial of Jesus, as some Jews have, as though it is basically historical but wrong in its details; such seems the approach of Solomon Zeitlin in *Who Crucified Jesus?* He contends that there were two Sanhedrins, a religious one and a political one, and that it was the latter, not the former, which condemned Jesus. But is it not equally possible that the whole trial matter is without historical foundation and that to quibble about this or that bit of procedure quite irrelevant? That a Christian writer in Mark's time could speak of a Sanhedrin can fall short of confirming that Jesus stood trial before it; and the fictional embellishments added by Luke and Matthew to Mark may well be the clue to the fictional character of Mark's account.

The question of historical reliability inevitably intrudes into questions of literary appreciation. One can, moreover, either confront an item and see it from the standpoint of its content respectively in Mark, Matthew, and Luke, or, with its differences, study it as the form critics did, in isolation from the Gospel. For example, Mark and Matthew report that Jesus was rejected in the synagogue of his home city Nazareth, but they put this well along in their accounts; in Luke the rejection in Nazareth is moved to the very beginning of Jesus' adulthood, as if to imply that Jews rejected Jesus right from the start. The point of the speech attributed to Jesus in Luke is that the benefit which he is destined to bring is designed for Gentiles, not for Jews. Luke's alteration of Mark is very considerable, both in content and in position; we need to be restrained, in dealing with Luke's account, about giving assent to the opinion that this portrayal of Jesus reading Isaiah in the synagogue is a reflection of the practice of Jews in reading the prophetic books as *haphtara* selections. The broad congruency of some item in the Gospels with Jewish practice does not in itself establish historical reliability, and the circumstance that a Jew who has studied some Talmud sees a kindred atmosphere in the Gospels does not necessarily confirm the reliability of the Gospel item.

What must be borne in mind is that already in the earliest of the written Gospels the embellishment of incidents about Jesus presents us with a contradiction: the portrayal of a believable background, but questionable or even unbelievable incidents. These embellishments represent not only the growth of oral tradition, but also the deliberate, purposeful embellishments by the authors of the Gospels. The treatment by Luke of Mark in the matter of the synagogue in Nazareth is fully consistent with his treatment of the many other Marcan incidents which he uses. The characteristics of Luke's Gospel turn out to be found in his treatment of Marcan materials, and to be present in his form of the Q materials, and to be present also in those materials which occur only in his Gospel.[3]

I insist one must conclude from the foregoing that each of the Gospels has its own individuality, something which has long been noticed by Protestant scholars. Yet in some quarters there has existed, and still exists, a reluctance to recognize that, as the Gospels differ from each other, so necessarily do the portraits of Jesus differ. Christians in general incline to what might be formulated in this way, that the four Gospels give interpretations of the one Jesus. My own opinion goes in a different direction, for I believe that one gets from the Gospels not one Jesus but four.

This opinion derives from more than just the study of the Gospels. In the age of Jesus the portrait of Abraham was embellished by Philo, by Josephus, by a book named the Book of Jubilees, and, later, by the rabbis. The embellishments of Abraham's portrait were not at all restrained by the achieved high sanctity of Genesis, for the embellishers not only extended what was to be found in Genesis, but even felt free to go against passages that are clear and explicit; this is especially the case in the treatment of Genesis 12, the sojourn of Abraham in Egypt and his equivocation about Sarah's being his sister.

In the same vein, Chronicles used Samuel and Kings as a source, but scarcely with that fidelity and care that a scrupulous historian would employ. Similarly, there is a layer in the Book of Samuel which is in utter contradiction with another layer there; the one describes how Samuel willingly anoints the great man Saul as king, while the other treats Saul as a rascal and portrays Samuel as opposed to monarchy, fluent in denouncing it, and reluctantly acquiescing in anointing Saul. Again, the Five Books of Moses present contradictory and inconsistent materials about Moses, and the historical Moses is every bit as elusive a character as the historical Jesus.

What all the writings, Old Testament, New Testament, and the additional quasi-biblical literature, have in common is that history for them was not the quasi-science it tried to become in the nineteenth century, but was rather an interpretation of accepted but unproved events. No author in those days had a Ph.D. from a modern university, or worked in archives, or strove to present "the events as they really happened." For us to confront those authors on the plane of "pure" history is to expect what they neither intended nor were able to provide. It is a hopeless task to disentangle history from nonhistory in the narratives of the Tanak, or of the extra-biblical literature, or of the New Testament. We cannot be precise about Jesus. We can know what the Gospels say, but we cannot know Jesus. If our objective is an accurate history of Jesus, then we are more apt to find that the Gospels obscure than reveal him. The acute differences in the Gospels rise to impede a merely literary appreciation of them.

All the above could have been written by a liberal Protestant scholar. Each idea presented can be traced to a responsible Christian writer. It chances, however, that I have evolved over the years a set of views about the Gospels. These views emerge from regarding them as documents, not sacred documents, and from viewing them, naturally, quite detached from veneration. There are in the Gospels things which I admire, and things which I do not admire. For example, I admire without reservation Luke's literary skill; I do not admire what seems to me his, and only his, incredible account that Herod Antipas was present in Jerusalem in Jesus' last week. I admire the story of the widow's mite [4] (Mark 12:41–4), but I do not admire the twenty-third chapter of Matthew; not only do I not believe that this chapter is authentically in Jesus' words, but I am puzzled that Christians can read this chapter and still speak of Jesus as a kindly man.

There is this risk in the approach of "Bible as literature," that a negative response is necessarily admissible. Such, in my reading, occurs in the Gospel According to John. Here I find myself divided within myself. John is a most interesting Gospel, and it is quite difficult but fascinating to study. It is replete with unexpected allusiveness, and it has a wealth of nuances and overtones, and hence it is the reverse of superficial. To the extent that I am a student of Christian beginnings, I need to assess this Gospel as of surpassing importance; I believe also that its data about Jesus are quite as valuable, quite as reliable, as the data in the other Gospels. Let me admit that there is this problem for me in my being Jewish, that John portrays the opponents of Jesus unequivocally as "the Jews," and not as Pharisees and chief priests; John sets the Jew Jesus over and against the Jews. But even considered as literature, I find myself unattracted in any way to the Jesus of John. I miss what to me are requisite overtones of modesty and humility; the omniscience repels me somewhat, and to me, the labored way in which Jesus knows everything that will happen and seems to be acting out a predetermined timetable strikes me as an unexalted device. Similarly, I do not have a charitable view of the repeated procedure in John whereby the point of departure for the soliloquies is the imputed misunderstanding by people of that which seems crystal clear; here again the device pushes me off. The Jesus in John is an extreme example. But it is indicative of what is at stake in the difference between a Christian and a Jew.

A Christian reading the Gospels has an empathy with Jesus, but I find that I have only a sporadic empathy with the Gospels in general, and I warm up only to scattered items.

For, to speak quite plainly, to my mind the Gospels on the one hand and the Epistles of Paul on the other hand seem to me to be on two different levels. I simply do not see in the Gospels any special profundity and startling perceptiveness, or any tremendously acute religious insight, surpassing other sacred literature. They are human, they are occasionally touching, they are here and there engaging. Since they are like anthologies of rabbinic anecdotes, I find myself quite often in full accord with some act of Jesus', or some word attributed to him. Indeed where I am not repelled, as I am by Matthew 23 with its cruel words, I find myself attracted and acquiescent, but not more so than by other edifying literature. I do not find in myself a feeling that the Gospels are superlative either as literature or as religious documents. They are for me antiquarian materials absorbing to study, but I cannot in any honesty evaluate them as superior to a simple book like Ruth, or IV Maccabees (an extraordinarily beautiful book), or Plato's *Symposium*, or Goethe's *Faust*, or Dostoyevsky's *Crime and Punishment*. If I felt that I knew more about Jesus than I do, I would be able to verify, or reject, a conjecture that the Gospels do not rise to the level of Jesus. I do not, then, find myself among the admirers of the Gospels as literature, and it would be false for me to pretend that I do.

Would a Jewish reader who is not a serious student react in a similar way? I believe that enough Jews have reported a like reaction to me to enable me to generalize that Jews do not share in a literary appreciation of the Gospels, that they wonder at the high assessment which non-Jews give them. They too seem to feel that somehow the Gospels fail to do justice to the figure of Jesus as they encounter it in its reflection in the hearts and minds of their Christian neighbors. To a Jew, reading as sympathetically as he is able, the Gospels create a bewilderment, not an appreciation. I can report that many a Jew, prior to reading the Gospels, has an estimate of them which the actual reading reduces.

I published an article in which I set forth the following opinion. For Matthew to have used Mark, but to have nevertheless composed a new and different work, implies that Matthew was dissatisfied with Mark; so too Luke, in his use of Mark, and so too if, as I believe, Luke used Matthew as a source. I cited next the opinion of a scholar, Ernest Colwell, that John wrote in dissatisfaction with, and in a desire to supplant, Mark, Matthew, and Luke; and I cited some passages from the Church fathers that John's Gospel had encountered some hostility in the early Church.

What this meant to me, and still means, is that the chore of writing an acceptable Gospel was fraught with great difficulties. I proposed that there was in the New Testament a Fifth Gospel calculated by its author to avoid the difficulties encountered by the four existing Gospels (and by others no longer extant), and this was the Epistle to the Hebrews. What had awakened me to this theory was a passage in Titus 1:14, which denounced "Jewish myths," and one in I Timothy 1:4, which asperses "myths and endless genealogies." If to some Christians, genealogies were idle, then the first thing which came to my mind was the genealogies in Matthew and Luke. As to the "myths," these seemed to me to be the warp and woof of the Gospels, and they were labeled "Jewish" only to disparage them. That is to say, it seems reasonable to my mind that early Christians did not necessarily approve of every Gospel that was written, and we know that in some quarters John was disapproved. I questioned whether the Gospels elicit admiration through their form and content, or rather through the centuries of their adulation after four of them became canonical. None of the anecdotes of the Gospels reappears in Hebrews; instead, we are there told that the Christ was "without father, without mother, and without genealogy." Moreover, certain of the Church fathers encountered in the canonical Gospels difficulties which they dispelled only through artificial allegory. I expressed my opinion that it is the almost eighteen centuries of the adulation of the Gospels which invests them with a character they do not possess, at least not for me.

The Epistles of Paul lack the homey anecdotes of the Gospels. I find in Paul, uncongenial as I find some of what he wrote (for example, his attitude toward marriage and sex relations), a challenging mind, a profoundly sensitive perception, a remarkably fluent and poetic pen, and hence a level which to me is far above the achievement of Matthew, Mark, Luke, or John. I am aware that Paul's writings are quite different from the Gospels; however, in recognizing the difference in form I am unable to place the Gospels on that same high level on which I willingly place Paul.

I shall be misunderstood if I am interpreted as scorning the Gospels; I am only commenting on the Gospels *as literature,* not on the Gospels as objects of study for a knowledge of early Christianity. I would add also that it is not alone for the Jewish reader that the Gospels present something of a problem, but also to the modern mind of whatever background. That great New Testament scholar, Rudolf Bultmann, whom I mentioned above (p. 95), is the leading mind and spirit behind a continental theological movement. His movement has awakened substantial opponents. It is called the "demythologizing school." It is Bultmann's judgment that the basic Christian message is tenable and proper; he contends, however, that as this message is couched in the New Testament it is so tied to the "mythology" of the Graeco-Roman world of 1900 years ago as to be both unintelligible and unacceptable to modern man. He proposes, therefore, that a task of Christianity is to reformulate its message so as to be able to capture the mind and the allegiance of modern man.

To the modern Jewish reader, the Gospels as literature seem destined to evoke resistance, to spur refutation. It has been my experience that, although I have tried to write sympathetically in introducing Jews to the Gospels, and have tried to assess in as balanced and detailed a way as I could the tension and dramatic nature of Mark, the systematic regularity and coherence of Matthew, and the genuinely artistic skill of Luke, still Jewish readers tell me that they fail to see what I have tried to persuade them to see.

Yet religious documents call for an assessment quite different from the merely literary, and there is the danger even among scholars that an overpreoccupation with analysis can obscure the inherent tenor of a document. To stop short at the literal is as grievous an offense to proper understanding as to ignore the literal, for the person who reads religious writings needs to push on to try to grasp the intent behind the document. For example, the rabbinic literature at its best never rises to the heights of the literary masterpieces of the Tanak, such as Job, Psalms, and the great literary prophets. There are, however, innumerable passages in which the rabbinic literature possesses a perception and a loftiness which vie with the best in the Tanak. He who judges the rabbinic literature only on its external form, or on its legalism, can miss what the rabbinic literature is truly saying, for its eloquence lies in the flashes of insight wherein content triumphs over form. Moreover, the proper interpreter never loses sight of the question, what is it to which the rabbinic literature is dedicated? What is it trying to tell us? Religious literature is always an effort to give expression to that which usually defies precise expression, for in religious literature men essay to express ideas and intuitions which often fail to fit into articulate words. Religious emotion tends to poetry, not to prose, and he is a dull student of religious literature who abstains from trying to grasp the poetry latent even in the most pedestrian of religious writing. The cultured Jew and the Christian owe to the literature of paganism, or Mohammedanism, or Buddhism the obligation to try to grasp the latent intent, even when they feel themselves outside, alien to, the tradition which has begotten the literature.

We Jews are outsiders to the New Testament, for it is not ours. Yet there is a sense in which this inevitable "outsidedness" that makes us stumble over the literal can itself be the clue to recognition of kinship. The very differences point to the paradox of the inherent core of Jewishness in the Christian literature, and this core is discernible however unsatisfying the Gospels may seem to us, and however we are persuaded by the scholars that this or that item is Hellenistic or pagan in origin.

The recognition of that core of Jewishness emerges when one proceeds to ask the searching questions which transcend the petty details, when one begins to inquire into the broad, telling question of what this Christian literature is all about. To inquire, what are the Gospels basically saying? is a more significant question than whether Jesus journeyed to Jerusalem southward through Galilee to Jerusalem, or eastward across the Jordan, southward, and then westward across the Jordan. To inquire, what is the true import of the Epistles? is beyond the necessary inquiry of whether or not Paul wrote all the Epistles attributed to him. The profound questions, in short, deal with the quintessence of the documents of the New Testament, not with those details which can often block understanding instead of promoting it.

What I am here about to say could be formulated in a variety of ways. I choose to speak of three great themes about which the Jewish literature, Tanak and Talmud, revolve. I see these same three themes as the collective pivot around with Christianity revolves.

The first of these is the question, is there such a thing as the will of God? Religious literature never poses this as a question, but invariably assumes its existence. That there is a will of God is the axiom of Judaism as of Christianity; it is the axiom that God exists and that there is a way which He espouses and approves, and a way which He discountenances. This theme is central in the Tanak, in the Prophets, and it is the leading motif of the Pentateuch. It is the song sung by the Psalmist, and it is the substance of the tremendous issues raised in the Book of Job. So also is this the theme which binds together the disparate writings of the New Testament, wherein a variety of men expressed this common conviction in differing ways. These writings have bequeathed to the modern age partly overlapping but partly discordant inferences drawn from the central convictions. The discordances, however, real as they are, tend to shrink in significance as mere details when they are weighed in the light of the central convictions. I describe this conviction about the will of God as Jewish; it is at the heart of all the ancient Jewish writings; it is also at the heart of Christian writings.

The second theme is the question, can man know the will of God? I doubt that any ancient religious writing ever proceeded from any conviction but that man can and does know that will. The issue is not the philosophical question of whether the will of God is truly knowable or not. That question has been raised in a variety of ways, and might well be appropriate to some other occasion, in some other context. Here it suffices that we see that that which is central in Judaism, and centrally Jewish in Christianity, is the firm conviction that man can and does know the will of God, because God has revealed it to him. The ancient Jewish and Christian writings provide ample testimony that one man's claim that he knew the will of God was distasteful and incredible to other men—that is why allusions are so frequent to false prophets and false teachers. Yet the conviction that man can know the will of God animates every paragraph of the ancient writings, Jewish and Christian. Indeed, so essentially Jewish is this motif that it takes in its Christian form the assertion that the Christian knowledge of God's will differs from the Jewish only in that as its continuation it is the more recent and more climactic knowledge. The Christian writings [5] not only do not reject the heritage of Judaism, but claim it as their very own, even to the extent of dispossessing the Jews of it. The Christian attitude toward that ancient revelation was affirmative, but it went on to ask, as it were, what has God been doing and what has been His will since that remote age of Moses at Sinai? To this question the Christians gave the answer that *recently*, in the days of Pontius Pilate, God had newly revealed Himself in Christ, and that this revelation was in unbroken continuity with the antecedent Jewish revelation. A Jew does not share this conviction any more than a Christian shares the Mohammedan conviction which came even later; yet a Jew should be able to discern that what Christianity is laying claim to is its right to the Jewish revelation. Christianity is essentially Jewish in its view that it has been granted to know the will of God.

The third theme is this, can man, knowing the will of God,

abide by it? Both Judaism and Christianity have asserted that man can, and should. They have disagreed on how man can achieve his conformity with the will of God; on many subjects, however, they have been in natural agreement. In social ethics, the two have agreed on goals and objectives, an agreement well nigh, though not quite, total; for example, I know nothing in Judaism which parallels the Christian counsel to turn the other cheek. Yet if there is some slight difference in emphasis at this one point, the social ideals are nevertheless synonymous. It is in answering the question *how* can man fulfill the will of God that a strand in Christianity is the antithesis of the Jewish way. Jews prescribed that man should execute the will of God through fidelity to revealed laws and regulations. Paul, on the other hand, believed that regulations could and would impede man's fidelity to God's will, and he proposed "faith," rather than "works" of the Mosaic Law. While in many areas motifs and concerns in Judaism and Christianity run along parallel lines, Paul's view and that of the main lines of Jewish tradition are here antithetical and are irreconcilable with each other. In the unfolding ages, Christianity often receded from Paulinism but sporadically returned to emphasize him, with the consequence that, in periods of emphasis, antithesis rather than similarity marked the traditions off from each other. Indeed, it is the Pauline element in Christianity which is the principal barrier to a Jew's comprehension of Christianity and to a Christian's comprehension of Judaism. Yet even in the case of Paul, I could hope that Jews, without abandoning either convictions or the inherited values of rabbinism, would try to discern in him the tremendous effort of a gifted Jew to answer the question, how can man execute God's will? Paul is Jewish, not only by birth, but because the question essential to Judaism, the question *how*, is what preoccupies him. We Jews should notice not so much the answers Paul gives—these are foreign to us—but his question, which is part of the matrix of Judaism.

Paul is by no means all of Christianity. Other New Testament writings contain motifs quite close to our Judaism, and at the same time they express concerns remote from it. It is certainly not the province of the Jew to agree with the New Testament concerns, but, on the other hand, it is surely not asking too much of the cultured citizen of the modern world to try to discern the nature of the Christian quest for how a man can do the will of God.

To the modern historian, including the Christian historian, the history of Christianity is considerably checkered, even in areas outside the Christian impingement on Jews. People seldom are completely God-intoxicated, and often people who boast of a loyalty to God have been singularly remiss. The ancient prophets enable us to see some examples of Jewish failure, and voices less ancient, though sturdy and eloquent, have spoken from within Christianity about Christian failure. Yet there have been in both traditions achievements and successes, and we Jews should not allow ourselves to be blind to Christian attainments.

Success or failure are quite possibly relative terms, and possibly involve subjective judgment. I confess that I have much less interest in passing judgment on Christian achievements or failures than in trying to grasp what Christianity is. Out of this personal disposition comes my conclusion that the Christian writings, Gospels and Epistles, represent a noble effort on the part of an offshoot of Judaism to formulate and reformulate in their way the themes inherent in and derived from Judaism.

The Christian way is not mine, nor are their answers mine. But I find no difficulty in seeing magnitude in a tradition not my own, and in discerning in that tradition a profound groping for God in a way different from my way. To discern such things is to view Christian Scriptures from the outside, but in the way in which I have often wished that Christians could see and discern the rabbinic literature. It means to see the writings beyond the mere details, beyond the merely literal, and to see in them the just claim that they possess humanistic values.

Notes

1. A minority of responsible Christian scholars do contend that it is a fiction.

2. In Hebrew poetry, "parallelism" often provides the double statement of a single matter. Zechariah 9:9 tells that the king will enter "riding on a colt, the foal of an ass." Matthew mistakenly interprets this to mean two animals.

3. I am among those who deny that there was a Q, for I prefer to believe that the correspondence between Matthew and Luke in the non-Marcan material results from Luke's having used Matthew as well as Mark as a source.

4. "She, out of her poverty, has put in everything she had, her whole living." The story is found also in Luke 21:1–4, but it is absent from Matthew and John.

5. One must except the marginal gnostics, whom the developing Church rejected for rejecting the Jewish revelation.

CHAPTER 6 · Toward a Jewish Attitude
to Christianity

The formulation of a balanced and affirmative Jewish attitude to
Christianity is fraught with difficulties that do not inhere respecting religions distant from each other. Early Christianity was a
Judaism; within a century after the death of Jesus it was a separate religion. It was critical of its parent, and hostile to it, and
elicited from its parent reciprocal criticism and hostility. Moreover, it developed a theological view which, in due course, became translated into economic, political, and social restrictions,
and which included confiscation of property, persecutions of extreme violence, and expulsions and deportations. Are these matters merely reflections of transitory historical occasions, or are
they essential in Christianity? Are they the accident of history, or
are they necessarily the warp and woof of Jewish-Christian
relations?

When we look in the New Testament at the criticism made of
Judaism, we can see it as presenting in the Gospels something

quite different from what it presents in the Epistles of Paul. The Gospels portray Jesus in controversy with his contemporaries. One subject of controversy is the criticism ascribed to Jesus of the religious sincerity of his contemporaries. A controversy on the Sabbath occurs in Mark 2:23–28, Matthew 12:1–8, and Luke 6:1–5. The disciples of Jesus pluck ears of grain on the Sabbath; Jesus cites an incident from I Samuel 21:1–6, in which David because of necessity violated certain regulations about Temple procedures (namely, eating dedicated food lawful only for priests to eat). His conclusion is that "the Sabbath was made for man, not man for the Sabbath." He then healed a man with a withered hand on the Sabbath, justifying it through the rhetorical question, "Is it lawful on the Sabbath to do good or to do harm, to save life or to kill?" [1]

In the controversy over the washing of hands (Mark 7:1–23 and Matthew 15:1–20) the opponents allege that some of the disciples of Jesus eat with unwashed hands, trespassing requirements elaborated in the oral revelation. Jesus does not deny the allegation; he retorts that the oral revelation at points contravenes the written revelation, and hence he charges that the oral revelation, a human development, contravenes God's law.

But as Jesus proceeds, he sets forth the principle that what defiles man cannot be what goes into him, but what comes out from him. The effect of this declaration is to repudiate [2] the Mosaic food laws found in Leviticus 11 and Deuteronomy 14.

The fact is that the Gospel materials do not provide a full, crystal-clear reflection of Jesus' attitude to the Law of Moses and to the oral law. Nowhere in the Gospels is there a clear adoption of the view of Paul that the Law was an impediment to righteousness, and hence superseded. The nearest approach is in the matter of the legality of divorce. Here the Pharisees quote Moses as having permitted it. Jesus concedes that there is a Mosaic permission, but he says, first, that Mosaic law permitted divorce "for your hardness of heart," he then proceeds to prohibit it (Mark 10:1–12). In Matthew 19:1–12 we read that prior to Moses there was no divorce, as if to imply that Jesus, in prohibiting it, was only reverting to pre-Mosaic conditions. Luke lacks a direct parallel; but Luke 16:18 portrays Jesus as equating with adultery the case of a man who divorces and remarries, or of one who marries a divorced woman.

Proceeding to a different level, the Gospels are replete with epithets of hypocrisy addressed by Jesus to his contemporaries. Matthew 23:23–26 and Luke 11:39–48 denounce scribes and Pharisees for hypocrisy in that they observe the external minutiae but neglect the weightier matters of "law, justice, and mercy, and faith." In its ordinary meaning, an allegation of hypocrisy challenges not the validity of the commandment being observed, but the good faith of the observer. Jesus in the controversies just noted (if they are historically authentic) is at variance with fellow Jews rather than with his inherited Judaism. In the matter of divorce, for Jesus to have been more rigorous than Moses did not directly contravene him. Only in the vague statement about food laws is Jesus at variance with his inherited Judaism.

I confess that I am not deeply troubled at, or resentful of, these imputations of hypocrisy, in the way that other Jewish commentators have been. Hypocrisy does occur universally in religions, even Christianity, and I do not feel called on to defend the Jews of Jesus' time for the hypocrisy alleged by Jesus. What amuses me, and occasionally annoys me, is an assessment of Judaism by some individual Christian that implies that Judaism by its mere nature lends itself to hypocrisy in a way in which it is implied that Christianity by its nature does not. The parable of the mote and the beam could well apply here.

But when we turn to the controversies in the Gospels over the role of Jesus, we are in a totally different situation. Here Jesus is at variance with both Jews and Judaism. He attributes to himself the prerogative of forgiving sins (Mark 2:1–12); the Sabbath controversy ends with these words: "So the Son of Man is Lord even of the Sabbath" (Mark 2:28 and parallels); the leaders question him on the source of his authority, but he does not tell them what it is (Mark 11:27–33 and parallels). Surprisingly, the Gospels are relatively scanty in materials involving the Pharisees and Jesus in a discussion of his role. Rather, the Gospels are written from the standpoint that his opponents never understood him and their hatred of him was blind malice. Hence, the Gospels lack a clear view as to the origin of Jewish hostility to Jesus. Indeed, when one reads Mark, he is struck by the supposition, prior to the events of the last week of Jesus' life, that Jesus was greatly welcomed by the Jewish masses, and it was only the leaders who are against him. Thus, at Jesus' entry into Jerusalem he was hailed by the onlookers (Mark 11:8–10); the chief priests were fearful of joining an issue with him "for they feared him, because all the multitude was astonished at his teaching" (Mark 11:18). Luke's version (Luke 19:48) reads: "All the people hung upon his words."

We are, hence, quite unprepared for the ascription to the multitude of a completely altered attitude, for none of the Gospels describes the process of change, nor even suggests any basis for it. Perhaps this is merely oversight; or perhaps the writers of the Gospels merely followed a bent to which I shall return a little later.

In sum, respecting the criticism by Jesus of Judaism, we are unable to see any clear picture of any profound distance between Jesus and his fellow Jews; we get only hints at such differences which might be called differences of principle. What is completely clear, however, is the repeated hostility, ranging from his allegations of wrong accentuations and hypocrisy through merciless denunciation; "vipers" would seem to be the favorite label. In Paul's Epistles, on the other hand, the criticism of Judaism is on principle, namely, that the Laws of Moses are a wrong vehicle for attaining righteousness, and are in fact an obstacle to that attainment. I do not suppose that we Jews, however faithful or unfaithful we might personally be to the Laws of Moses or the rabbinic *halacha*, will ever subscribe to Paul's views on the Law. Indeed, we will wonder at a Christendom which scorns Jewish legalism but has developed its own. We Jews will scarcely concede that Gospel is superior to Law, or that "faith" is superior to "works." Insofar as Christians, especially Protestants, make such an allegation, we may be trapped into replying in kind. Trapped, for these matters do not lend themselves to objective weighing, and thus they are subjectively the partisan sentiments of parti-

sans. Such judgments result from a lack of understanding and con-
tribute to perpetuating it.

The events of the last week of Jesus' life contain both implicit and
explicit allegations that Jews were responsible for the death of
Jesus. The epithet "Christ killer" has pursued Jews relentlessly in
Christian lands, and sticks and stones and more lethal instru-
ments have accentuated the name-calling.

What shall a Jew say to himself and his children about this
age-old Christian charge that the Jews, we Jews and not our ancestors alone, are "Christ killers"? What we might say to ourselves
would involve several steps. We might say, first, that the accounts
in the Gospels on the one hand are so replete with legend and
tendentiousness and Old Testament paraphrases as to reduce
almost to the vanishing point any substantial historical value.
What, for example, happened to the abundance of people resurrected with Jesus as Matthew alone related it? How reliable is an
account in which the incident occurs of a severed ear miraculously restored? How authentic are accounts of a trial which contain so many contradictions and differences, such as two trials by
the Sanhedrin in Mark, against one in Matthew and Luke, and
none in John? What confidence can there be in Luke's version
which alone in the Gospel narratives makes Herod Antipas present in Jerusalem for Pilate to send Jesus to him? Did the trial and
execution, as Mark, Matthew, and Luke relate, take place on
Passover, which is against all Jewish practice and, hence, against
all likelihood? Or was it the day before Passover, as John relates,
at a time of the day later than the other accounts relate and without the darkening of the sun? Cannot one discern the palpable
shift of responsibility from Pilate to the Jews, through the patent
devices by which Pilate is portrayed as reluctantly giving in to
Jewish malevolence? Can the fact that the crucifixion was a
Roman punishment, not a Jewish one, be so glossed over as to
exculpate the Romans entirely, as Christian literature does, and
not absolve the Jews at all? What shall we make of the circumstance that the Gospel accounts clarify to us why Romans would
will the death of Jesus, but leave someone like me uninformed,

even mystified, as to why Jews would have willed it? The Gospels show me no persuasive basis on which Jews as Jews would have leveled an accusation against a fellow-Jew; all that I read in the Gospels is a vague charge of "blasphemy," a charge unaccompanied by any broad effort to adduce relevant particulars. I can see in the Gospels what Jews could have rejected, and what they could have, as Jews, disliked. I cannot see in the Gospels themselves, as I can see in Paul's Epistles with his scorn of Moses' laws, what Jews as Jews would have resented so bitterly. I can understand the Roman motives; from the Gospels I detect no convincing Jewish motive. I believe that the shift of responsibility is patent, is motivated, and that we Jews have been made to pay for what Romans did.

Yet what have we Jews really accomplished by such a scrutiny of the Gospels as historical sources? Perhaps we have thereby persuaded ourselves of our innocence; perhaps, if we are willing to read modern Christian commentators, we can learn, happily, that some Christians on their own have achieved this same persuasion; but many, perhaps most, Christians will never be persuaded either of our ancestors' innocence or of ours.

Or, on the other hand, we can ask ourselves this, cannot Christians come to some clarity on one issue? If the death of Jesus was the universal benefit they hold it to be, then why attach blame, whether on the Jews or on the Romans, for causing the benefit? Again, if, as the Gospels, especially John, suppose, Jesus knew and predicted long in advance that the particular events would happen, and the events were neither a surprise nor a defeat, then were not the events merely a working out of some antecedently arrived at divine schedule? If it was part of a divine schedule, then why blame mere men for acting out the preordained human role?

Or, to take a different tack, why is it that the earliest Christian writings, the Epistles of Paul, which are so critical of Jews for rejecting Paul's view of the Christ, say little or nothing about Jewish blame for the crucifixion?[3] Would not Paul, so blunt in denouncing Jews, have been eager, even zealous, to throw the charge of Christ-killer at them? I think that in his occasional intemperate moments he might well have done so. Yet his Epistles notably lack this. The conclusion seems necessary that the allegations arose after Paul's time.

Perhaps we might be willing to say to ourselves that it is not at all impossible that some Jews, even leading Jews, recommended the death of Jesus to Pilate. We are averse to saying this to ourselves, for so total has the charge been against us that we have been constrained to make a total denial. Yet if we admit— admit, not confess!—that some Jews were involved, then why blame us all, both then and now? And since Jesus was a Jew, is it not more reasonable to say that *people* killed Jesus, than to put the statement as though Jesus were not a Jew, but his opponents were? Is it not equally unfair to say *the* Americans killed Lincoln and Kennedy?

These are the kinds of things we might say to ourselves. To Christians we can say very little. Do they charge us with responsibility for the death of Jesus? Or do they perchance mean that our stubborn abstention from sharing their theology is what really makes them regard us as Christ-killers? Is it consistent with Christian love and forgiveness to maintain an unforgiving hatred of Jews? Or does Christianity lessen itself, indeed, cheapen itself, by harboring hatred for anyone? As a Jew, I openly disavow and reject the occasional minor motifs recurrent in Judaism of hatred of Gentiles; these motifs lessen and cheapen Judaism. The anti-Jewish motif in Christianity appears to me to be greater in scope and deeper in intensity than the comparable motifs in Judaism which I find abhorrent.

My parents fled Eastern Europe to escape pogroms which began with the ringing of church bells. My mother used to say that even after decades in America the ringing of church bells could still occasionally frighten her. When I was a boy, I was more than once described as Christ-killer, especially by gangs of boys. I recall a few occasions when such gangs chased me; I don't recall if they ever caught me. Most Jews my age have had at least the former experience.

My two oldest boys belong to a Boy Scout troop which has its headquarters at the near-by Episcopal Church.[4] Not one of my sons has ever spoken to my wife or me about "Christ-killers." Apparently none of them has experienced what for me was no unusual occurrence. Will they some day experience it? And if they have children, will those children experience it?

This is in the hands of Christians, not of us Jews.

How shall we assess for the future the dismal record of the past? The persecutions of Jews took place; the expulsions of Jews took place. They were real; they are documented. To repeat, are they the essence of Christianity, or only reflections of particular historical occasions? Is the future relationship of Judaism and Christianity to be dominated, even shaped, by a past which is not in man's capacity to alter? Or is it possible that we can today understand this past better than we once did?

In approaching such a question, we might begin with what is practical and observable: In many an American city a concern for the public welfare brings Jews and Christians into common endeavor, and finds them often united in purpose and goals, and even in co-operative enterprises. The theological differences do not necessarily impede such co-operation, though often Jews and Christians can in general have divergent approaches to a particular issue, as, for example, prayer in the public schools. But the activities of the Community Chest or the "United Appeal" show that there is in this country already a rather long history of Jewish and Christian collaboration. Indeed, Jews today are to be found on the board of directors of strictly Christian enterprises, such as Catholic colleges and YMCA's, and, on the other hand, Christian clergymen have volunteered their services on behalf of Jewish enterprises, such as Zionist endeavors, or have contributed moneys to Jewish hospitals.

The fact is that in the past century, and particularly in the past three decades, Christians have taken leadership in opposition to the persecutions by Hitler and to the discriminations and disheartening manifestations of prejudice. Christian educators have shown a willingness, indeed, an eagerness, to eliminate from Christian education, especially from religious school textbooks, any expression which would seem to reflect on Jews as a group and which would encourage or justify a Christian child in a hostile or even inimical attitude to Jews. A good many Christian denominations have created study plans whereby Christian youngsters can gain an affirmative appreciation of Judaism; many a Christian summer camp has a rabbi on its staff, and in virtually every American city Christian children are brought in groups by their teachers to visit and tour synagogues. In the past it was primarily Protestants to whom these references applied; in the past five years it has come to apply to Roman Catholics as well.

The fact is that in the past century in the United States, the historic mutual animosities of Christianity and Judaism have given way to what is no less than a reversal of the past. Anti-Jewish sentiment in Western Europe had undergone in the nineteenth century a shift from a religious to a quasi-racial basis. As a consequence, Nazi anti-Semitism was paralleled by an equally uncompromising hostility to Christianity. The Nazis, as the tragedy of Jews in Europe confirms, did not treat *Jews* and *Christians* in the same way; but there is significance in their common antipathy to *Judaism* and *Christianity*. But the saving of Jewish lives in Holland and France, and even in Germany, and the unique experience in Denmark, which saved virtually all of its Jewish community by secretly leading it to safety in Sweden, illuminated the changed situation; the descendants of persecutors became rescuers.

One should not exaggerate the scope or intensity of the historic reversal by closing his eyes to abiding remnants of Christian hostility to Jews and to its Jewish counterparts. There are still Christians, even clergymen, who see in the New Testament not only a continued sanction but even an imperative to hate Jews, and I get the impression that to such Christians the New Testament is meaningful only in that one way. It is such people who have given Jews the distorted notion that the New Testament has only the one single theme, that of anti-Jewish feeling. From time to time we Jews have had to pause to wonder how such Christians could reconcile their belief in a God of love with their conclusion that one must, in the name of Jesus, hate.

Granted, then, that there remain both on the Christian and the Jewish sides recurring vestiges of the age-old antipathy, the statement remains nevertheless true that Christianity and Judaism have in the past century and a half, particularly in the United States, reversed their historical approaches to each other.

Perhaps this startling reversal makes it possible to see in some greater perspective the origin and the true significance of the animosities of the past. For example, I contend that, for those who wish so to use it, the New Testament is the supreme source for anti-Jewish feeling, but that this is the case only because sources even more virulent are not so readily known to modern man. The second, third, and fourth Christian centuries witnessed anti-Jewish writings that exceed even what is in the New Testament. Such writings frequently bore the title, "Against the Jews." They reflect an unhappy universal phenomenon in the long history of the thread of Judeo-Christian developments, that the rise of some new movement promptly pitted it against its forebear, so that the common heritage was overlooked in the ascendancy of a restricted number of items, and the new movement justified its novelties by a merciless criticism of the old. The Christian diatribes against Jews and Judaism were recapitulated in the same way by the Lutherans against the Catholics, and by the Dissenters against the Church of England. The tragedy for Jews has been that the late New Testament literature partakes of this universal recrimination and abuse. What Protestants wrote about Catholics in the sixteenth century is known only to the student of history, but the New Testament reflection of this common religious animosity makes it readily available and known and readily transmittable from generation to generation.

As to these Christian attacks on Jews and Judaism, perspective demands that we notice that denunciation and abuse were part of the customs and the modes of writing of the age. The New Testament contains denunciations of Christian heretics that are as abusive as the denunciations of Jews; and when we go into the Church fathers, we can see that Tertullian or Irenaeus could write as bitterly against fellow-Christians of different opinions as against Jews. Indeed, the "apologetic" literature of the early

Church treated the Greek tradition, that vaunted heritage, that pillar of modern education, to exactly the same kind of shattering denunciation. In context, the lamentable Christian writings against Jews are part and parcel of the lamentable way in which people wrote. Jews too have indulged in this kind of literary disgrace, as, for example, in the opinions which Rabbanites and Karaites expressed against each other; in the controversies between the eighteenth-century Hassidim and their "opponents," the "Misnagdim"; in the mutual compliments of the Reform and Orthodox Jews, or of Orthodox and Conservatives; in the mutual recriminations of Zionist and anti-Zionist. In the United States today there are Christians who denounce the National Council of the Churches of Christ, which is an association of large, significant, eminent, Protestant bodies, as an un-Christian, Communist-front entity!

The wry observation needs to be made that, in religious animosities, the depth of the feeling usually reflects the relative closeness to each other of the antagonized partisans. In the case of the Christian polemics against Jews, then, the particular denunciations need some evaluation as products of particular ages and of the disposition to denounce, and the closeness of Christianity to Judaism.

Somewhat similarly, the Christian persecution of Jews needs the perspective of the tendency in various ages of people to persecute. One misreads Jewish history in respect to Christian persecution if he neglects to notice how Christians persecuted each other. The fourth century witnessed the heresy of the "Arians," and the resultant persecutions continued for centuries. The persecution of the Albigensian "heretics" of southern France, in the thirteenth century, was at least as cruel as the persecution of any Jewish community. The cruelties wrought on Jews in the Rhineland in the First Crusade (1096–99) were at least matched by the horrors inflicted in the Fourth Crusade (1202–04) on the Byzantine Christians in the pillaging and destruction of Constantinople.

Or, to take another example, there arose in the fifteenth century the assumed need to persecute witches. In the sixteenth century, a number of popes urged such criminal persecution; it seems reasonable, though, to conclude that Protestants, especially Calvinists, exceeded Catholics in the zeal to persecute witches. In the seventeenth century thousands of women were put to death on the charge in Germany and France, while hundreds died in England. In Salem, Massachusetts, nineteen witches were hanged in 1622, and one was executed by "pressing."

Again, the Tower of London is famous, or notorious, as the place of confinement of some of the most eminent names in British history, many of whom went from the Tower directly to the execution block: Thomas More, Anne Boleyn, Catherine Howard, and Sir Walter Raleigh among them. Bedlam is the popular name of the Bethlehem Hospital in London, where the insane were treated as criminals rather than as sick people. The debtors' prison lasted in American federal law until 1800, but persisted in New York until 1828–32; Charles Dickens as a little boy shared with his father and family a sojourn in Marshalsea prison, where his father was confined for debt in 1815.

Slavery was first abolished in the Western World in two steps. First came the legal abolition of the slave trade, which was enacted by Denmark in 1792, by England in 1807, and by the United States in 1808. As for the millions already in slavery, the British House of Commons emancipated the slaves in all British colonies in 1833; slavery was abolished in the United States only through the Civil War, 1860–65.

The persecutions of Jews by Christians ought to be seen as one of the many horrors with which the history of mankind has been unduly filled, and it represents not so much a Christian characteristic as a human one. If one is inclined to put some special blame on Christianity, such blame should attach not so much to the fact of persecution but to the failure of Christendom to avert or eliminate it. Civilizations which boast that they are Christian scarcely merit the epithet if within them the conduct of affairs is no different from that of heathen lands.

No Jew who was already mature when Hitler came to power is as yet able to assess the significance of that greatest tragedy in mankind's history. The fact is that Jews were a special target of the Nazis, and that, broad as was the cruelty inflicted on the people of Poland, Russia, Holland, Belgium, and France, Jews suffered, if not numerically more, certainly more acutely and ineluctably. But only that Jew who mistakenly identifies Gentile with Christian has a basis for blaming Christians as such for the Nazi persecutions; it can suffice only to notice that Mr. Churchill and the late Mr. Roosevelt, professing Christians, led the successful opposition to Nazism.

At the present writing, a drama called *The Deputy* is running in London and Paris and has opened in New York. It is an indictment of Pope Pius XII for the alleged insufficiency of action on his part to forfend against Hitler's destruction of the Jews. The author is a Protestant. The play has provoked public disorders. Catholics have resented both the substance and the form of the imputations against Pope Pius. The form of the imputations has evoked the Catholic charge that the play is slanderous and bigoted; as to substance, the rebuttal has been made, in periodicals I have read, that Pius's alleged insufficiency of protest was deliberate strategy whereby the lesser of two evils was chosen; the Vatican was enabled through its chosen way to save more Jews than it could have saved through Pius's open intervention with the Nazis on behalf of the Jews.

I have no basis for an opinion on the play, nor, indeed, on the charges and rebuttals. What strikes me most forcibly is the common assumption, by both the Protestant playwright and his Catholic opponents, that the Christian conscience should not countenance the persecution of Jews. This assumption seems no issue whatsoever between the parties; the issue is whether the papacy did or did not do all that in the particular situation could have been done. That Christians are obligated to have concern for the welfare of Jews is a modern conclusion, the product of a new form and substance in Jewish-Christian relations.

It is a matter of record that, in the United States, Jews and Protestants, especially among the clergy, evolved a mutually affirmative approach many decades ago. Rabbis and ministers in our day so take this for granted that its novelty is long since gone and it is practiced with no surprise or self-consciousness. For decades Jews have lectured at Protestant divinity schools, and Protestants at Jewish seminaries.

The relation between Jews and Catholics has not been the same. In the United States the relationship was usually one of minimum contact and of almost no exchange. In the past five years this has changed, in reflection of the way in which Catholic-Protestant relations have changed.

Those who are acquainted with Jewish history are saddened by two incidents which necessarily affect Jewish attitudes toward the Catholic Church. One is the Mortara Affair. In Bologna in 1858 the Catholic nurse to the Jewish Mortara family had the baby, Edgar, secretly baptized when he was sick. A few years later Church authorities forcibly took the child from its parents, and the Church, despite appeals from all over the world, even from Catholics, never returned the child. Jews, understandably, speak of this as an act of official kidnaping.

The second incident is the Dreyfus Affair of 1894–1904. Dreyfus, a Jewish officer in the French army, was falsely accused of treason and convicted, and even after his innocence was established, it took a change of government for him to secure a new trial. At the second trial, despite the established facts, he was again condemned; the President of France granted him a pardon, and only a year later did a court quash the verdict and pronounce him innocent. The role of the Catholic Church in France in the public upheavals over the Dreyfus case was hostile not alone to Dreyfus but to Jews.

These two modern incidents are only part of a more general pattern in Jewish eyes in which a chief obstacle to the civic, political, and economic freedom of Jews has been the Catholic Church, and the evidence could be adduced, as from the Argentine, that the Church has included within it those who have exerted themselves to the disadvantage of Jewish rights. Americans also recall the name of Father Charles Coughlin, who, in the 1930's used a network hook-up on the radio to spread a modern version of medieval calumnies against the Jews, this at a time when Germany had gone Nazi.

Yet if Jews are keenly sensitive to the role of the Catholic

Church in reactionary movements, so have been many, many Catholics. There is little basis for doubt that one of the struggles of the Vatican Council is between those elements who wish to maintain the Catholic attitude relatively unchanged and those elements who are eager for the Church to shed its alignment with reactionary forces. Priests whom I know have impressed me as even more eager than Jews for the Church to disavow anti-Jewish hostility, not only by word but by example and by precept.

The action of the third session of the Vatican Council on November 20, 1964, in approving a statement on the Jewish people which the fourth session is expected to promulgate, possibly in 1965, is of great importance. That statement, overwhelmingly approved, is reported in the press as declaring that "what happened to Christ in His passion cannot be attributed to the whole [Jewish] people then alive, much less to that today." The declaration is highly significant, pointing as it does to beneficent results, especially in those parts of the world where these are needed so much more urgently than in the United States. The expected promulgation, and thereafter the sequels, can amount, hopefully, to the most important single development in the history of Jewish and Catholic relations.

To be sure, some Jews have expressed their dismay at the activities of Jewish organizations that are alleged, in my opinion with some basis, of having forsaken dignity and self-respect in their urging this action on Catholics. Other Jews have taken the stand that since Jews are, and always have been, innocent of the collective responsibility for the death of Jesus, the declaration is in the nature of an obligation, and hence one need not say thanks when what is merely an obligation is paid; while I believe that I can understand this latter attitude, I do not share in it, principally because I know the earnestness on the part of Catholics who have come to this high point not alone through a sense of obligation, but also through unassailably genuine magnanimity, and after extremely penetrating self-search and even self-accusation. I am impressed, moreover, by the vigor and dedication with which Catholic prelates, eager for the declaration, resolutely pressed to the high goal of this enlightened purpose and conviction. My acquaintance is limited to American Catholics; my experience has led me to have full confidence in their integrity, and I am moved to grasp in friendship the hand which they extend in friendship.

Theological differences, real, profound, and decisive, need not be barriers to mutual religious understanding. They can, indeed, serve as the means, when the will exists, of channeling the understanding into affirmative and constructive endeavors. This statement is by now a truism. But in the present context it has this relevancy, that my exposition of a basic theological divergency is for me no obstacle to my respecting Christianity, to my admiration for what I regard as its achievements, and to my willingness wholeheartedly to join with Christians in those co-operative ventures that violate neither their convictions nor my own. That Christians have beliefs about Jesus which I do not share does not inhibit me from acknowledging that there is a broad array of concerns which I do share with them: the welfare of man, the urgency of ethical and moral standards, the crying need for the uplift of man's spiritual life.

Early Christianity was a Judaism. It acquired its name, Christianity, about a half-century after the time of Jesus. Were it not for the accident of nomenclature, the distinctions between Judaism and Christianity, rooted in theology and fixed by diverse historical experiences, would not support the broad impression which endured so long, that they are total distinctions. They are not; the fact that Christianity was born within Judaism meant that it shared extensive common possessions. For it to have been ultimately distinguishable from Judaism meant that it developed motifs of its own. Judaism and Christianity have innately a large measure of overlap, and had Christianity not come to call itself Christianity, but retained its early terminology that it was indeed *the* Judaism, it would be unnecessary for the overlap to need pointing out.

The term Christianity in our age also represents diversities, for example, Protestantism and Catholicism, which are as basic in their own way as the differences between Judaism and Christianity. When we use the words Protestantism and Catholicism we unconsciously stress the areas of difference among Christians and glide over the Scripture common to them, the common sacred calendar, and common nuances so vital to communal organisms. So also, when we speak of Judaism and Christianity, we seem to stress the abiding differences and to glide over a common belief in God, a common ethic, and a common devotion to education and to charity. The Romans could not discern between Jews and Christians; perhaps a man from Mars would view Judaism and Christianity, even in our day, as more kindred than unrelated. If one rises above nomenclature, then, it is by no means incorrect to speak of Christianity as a Judaism. Indeed, of the many varieties of Judaism which existed in the days of Jesus, two alone have abided into our time, rabbinic Judaism and Christianity.

I am not a Christian; I do not share in those convictions which make Christians of men. Moreover, I am inextricably bound up in my Judaism. Yet I have no disposition to set the one against the other, and to make meaningless comparisons. I do not regard Judaism as objectively superior to Christianity nor Christianity to Judaism. Rather, Judaism is mine, and I consider it good, and I am at home in it, and I love it, and want it. That is how I want Christians to feel about their Christianity.

Wherever and whenever there is opportunity to collaborate with Christians, provided it can be done with full dignity and full candor, I am willing, even eager to do so. For me to harbor against my American Christian neighbor the accusation that he himself is responsible for what European Christians did to Jews in Spain in 1492 or in Poland in 1648 is no more reasonable, and no more laudable, than for my Christian neighbor to hold me or my children personally responsible for whatever minor participation some Jews may or may not have had in the death of Jesus. There can be no possible outcome from the perpetuation of outworn grievances except the creation of new ones, and nothing more misdirected than for American Jews and Christians to maintain an outmoded feud which is contrary to the explicit ideals of both.

For almost eighteen centuries Judaism and Christianity faced each other as enemies. In the past hundred years we have learned much that earlier centuries failed to learn. Perhaps we have now learned that, in a world of many currents and crosscurrents, Judaism and Christianity are not so much on opposite sides of the fence as on the same side. We are not so much opposed as we are different from each other, working in co-operation. The helmsmen of the craft of faith are of different persuasion, but through steering carefully across the currents and crosscurrents of troubled times their direction may well be toward a mainland of understanding, and thereby of blessing to humanity.

Notes

1. What is puzzling to Jewish students is that the Jewish attitude about the Sabbath as reflected in rabbinic Judaism is near to that ascribed to Jesus and remote from that ascribed to his opponents. Jews support the proposition that in matters of urgency—for example, life or death—the Sabbath regulations must give way.

2. If the controversy authentically represents the attitude of Jesus, then, in this particular, his attitude anticipated that of Paul. It is supposed by some Christian interpreters that this quasi-Pauline attitude, of nullifying Mosaic laws, represents an age after that of Jesus, and reflects Paul's influence.

While normative Jewish interpretation often drastically changed the sense and even the intent of a scriptural passage, such direct repudiation would imply that someone greater than Moses had arisen with authority to reject what Moses taught. Jews have not believed this to be the case.

Even those Jews of today who do not observe the dietary laws have never suggested that they have a divine sanction for this abstinence. Some Jews disregard the food laws merely for the inconvenience or for their, to them, meaninglessness; Reform or "liberal" Jews justify their disregard on the basis of historical development, suggesting that the laws are ancient tabus, no longer relevant to modern men.

That the Jewish food laws, and the requirement of handwashing, have both had beneficent hygienic effect has led to a common erroneous impression that hygiene was their purpose. It was not, but was instead a remarkably salutary by-product.

3. The chief and really the only passage in Paul's Epistles which touches on blame is I Thessalonians 2:15. It touches on a theme later amplified in Chris-

tian polemical writings to the effect that Jews *always* killed their prophets. The passage seems to some Christian scholars to be an interpolation from a time well after the age of Paul; some interpreters, however, regard the entire Epistle as not by Paul. To such questions there is no answer; the opinions cited underline the singular nature of this passage in the totality of Paul's attitudes.

4. It was very touching to us that when Charles earned the Ner Tamid award, which was given to him during a synagogue exercise, adult officials of the troop and some of the scouts attended the synagogue services to witness the achievement and to share in our pride in it.

BIBLIOGRAPHY

More has been written on Jesus, the Gospels, and the background of Christianity than on any other set of related subjects. The purpose of this brief bibliography is specific, namely to provide a list of books which can initiate the unacquainted into this complex and complicated field. I have mostly confined this list to books which go unmentioned in the text and which are scholarly by nature, though not all of them are technical books. The modes of scholarship differ, so that, as elsewhere, one encounters the shades of conservatism, extreme or moderate, and of liberalism, moderate or extreme; I selected for inclusion those books which seem to me to represent the approach of the scholars of the great American universities, that is, middle-of-the-road liberals. Also, I have felt it desirable to mention *The Bridge*.

The most useful encyclopedia is the *Interpreter's Bible Dictionary*, 4 volumes, New York, 1962. Many of the articles are of exceptionally high merit, and very, very few of them reflect condescension toward Judaism or Jews. Those that do (as for example, the article "Pharisees") are not so much hostile, as victims of the inability of some scholars to rise above their own parochialism. Since such writers start with the premise that Christianity is in its nature superior to Judaism, these articles are remarkably less condescending than they might have been. The keynote to the *Interpreter's Bible Dictionary* is its general soundness and its breadth; its chief deficiency is that it is less profound than it could have been. It was directed to a general audience such as ministers and rabbis rather than to technical scholars. A good many Jewish scholars were contributors.

As to the literature on the New Testament, two general introductions could be useful to Jewish readers. My own *A Jewish Understanding of the New Testament*, Cincinnati, 1956, is elementary. Some Christian readers have praised its clarity, but others, mostly Jews, have sometimes described it as very difficult reading. I suspect that at least in part the strangeness of the subject can make the book seem arduous to a Jewish beginner. The book has been properly criticized by some reviewers, especially the chapter on John, for its deliberate oversimplicity, and yet it is precisely this chapter which Jewish readers have informed me is insurmountably complex. A much more advanced book for the progressing reader is Morton S. Enslin, *Christian Beginnings*, New York, 1938. It is detailed and rather full, and written with true grace and felicity. The Jewish backgrounds are exceptionally well described, and sympathetically so. Clarence Tucker Craig, *The Beginning of Christianity*, New York, 1943, presents a good summary of the New Testament, oriented to history. Frederick C. Grant, *An Introduction to New Testament Thought*, New York, 1950, is excellent; the author is an unusually skillful and responsible teacher, adept at making difficult matters clear. Professor Grant discusses the material under headings such as God, Christ, Man, and the like. E. F. Scott, *Varieties of New Testament Religion*, New York, 1943, discusses this same material according to the segments of literature, relating the literature to different geographical and time factors in the New Testament age, with topics such as "The Religion of Paul," "The Moralists," "Western Christianity," and the like. Ernest William Parsons, *The Religion of the*

New Testament, New York, 1939, discusses the material largely in the sequence of the various New Testament writings. All three of these books overlap, but each is admirable and useful. Much more complex is Rudolf Bultmann, *Theology of the New Testament,* 2 volumes (Eng. trans.), London, 1958–59, but this work is suitable only for the advanced reader.

Two books by Charles Guignebert are to be commended to the student with a bent for history. His *The Jewish World in the Time of Jesus* (Eng. trans.), New York, 1959, predates the Dead Sea scrolls but is nevertheless not out of date. His *Jesus* (Eng. trans.), London, 1935, is marred for some Christian readers by his rigid and rigorous historical orientation, and it is therefore in great contrast to the books which blend piety and history. This is especially true regarding its tone, which seems to Christians, and to me, antagonistic to Christianity. A book far removed from these in character and manner is the excellent work by Henry C. Cadbury, *The Peril of Modernizing Jesus,* New York, 1937, which insists that Jesus was a Jew of the first century, not the twentieth. A useful book is Donald C. Ridelle, *Jesus and the Pharisees,* Chicago, 1928. Any serious research on the position of Jesus in Jewish writings must begin with a book in German by the Swedish scholar, Gösta Lindeskog, *Die Jesusfrage im neuzeitlichen Judentum,* Uppsala, 1938. A smaller book, somewhat on the same lines though not nearly as detailed, is Thomas Walker, *Jewish Views on Jesus,* London, 1931. Paul Winter, *On the Trial of Jesus,* Berlin, 1961, dealing with aspects of the trial, is for the technical scholar.

Many works have appeared on the lamentable history of Christian and Jewish relations. Conrad Moehlman, *The Christian-Jewish Tragedy, A Study in Religious Prejudice,* Rochester, N. Y., 1933, and Malcolm Hay, *The Foot of Pride,* Boston, 1950, are respective Protestant and Catholic approaches, and are marked by a repudiation of religious animosity. Both these works deal with the history rather than with the theological bases for the events. Some of the works of James Parkes seem to me to be stronger in the treatment of the medieval period than in the New Testament materials; his *Conflict of the Church and Synagogue,*

London, 1961, is a very important contribution. A somewhat curious book is Gregory Baum, *The Jews and the Gospel, A Re-examination of the New Testament*, London, 1961. Father Baum, of Jewish extraction, exonerates the New Testament itself of anti-Jewish sentiment, and ascribes it instead to the Church of the post-New Testament age. This exoneration strikes me as capricious, for it exhibits an interpretive manner which can equate black and white as the same color. Elsewhere, as in the pages of *Commonweal*, Father Baum has written eloquently and passionately against anti-Jewish sentiments, and he does so in this book also, so that my comment on his interpretive method is in the nature of a pedant's reservations. Father Baum was prompted to write especially by the deeply moving books of a French Jew, Jules Isaac. Isaac's *Jésus et Israel*, Paris, 1959, assembles many historical materials on the responsibility of Christianity in the history of Jewish suffering, while *The Teaching of Contempt* (Eng. trans.), New York, 1964, focuses on the anti-Jewish elements latent and explicit in Christian instruction.

A series entitled *The Bridge: A Yearbook of Judaeo-Christian Studies* first appeared in 1955. Not only is it under Roman Catholic auspices, but only Roman Catholics may appear in its pages. The editor, Father John M. Oesterreicher, is an apostate from Judaism. On page 9, Volume I, there appears a justification for terming this work a "dialogue"; this is apparently a reflection of the awareness that the editorial policy which excludes non-Catholics from representation in the writing merits its being called "dialogue" only through a most arrogant distortion of the plain meaning of the word. It has, happily, been possible for us Jews to be in dialogue with Catholics since the papacy of John XXIII, and hence being barred from the pages of *The Bridge* need not disturb us. While essays in *The Bridge* are occasionally urbane, the enterprise is a most uncivilized one, and Jewish scholars in abundance have expressed in writing a deep Jewish resentment of *The Bridge*.

Lastly, there is to be commended the excellent and penetrating study of religious instruction and religious animosity in Bernhard E. Olson, *Faith and Prejudice*, New Haven, 1963. It is an investigation into the contents of religious school textbooks, an investigation aimed at reflecting the contents and treatment of religious diversities and discords in them. An objective inquiry into the fact, Professor Olson's clear and calm text is admirable in its illumination and in its straightforwardness. If Jews may be disturbed by the amount of abiding anti-Jewish sentiment in Christian circles, the Olson study bears out how increasingly in Christian circles animosity toward Jews has receded, and in some Christian circles has been totally eliminated, from religious school textbooks.

INDEX OF SUBJECTS

INDEX OF SCRIPTURES

Spirituality of the Seasons

Autumn: A Spiritual Biography of the Season
Edited by Gary Schmidt and Susan M. Felch; Illustrations by Mary Azarian
Rejoice in autumn as a time of preparation and reflection. Includes Wendell Berry, David James Duncan, Robert Frost, A. Bartlett Giamatti, E. B. White, P. D. James, Julian of Norwich, Garret Keizer, Tracy Kidder, Anne Lamott, May Sarton.
6 x 9, 320 pp, 5 b/w illus., Quality PB, 978-1-59473-118-1 **$18.99**
HC, 978-1-59473-005-4 **$22.99**

Spring: A Spiritual Biography of the Season
Edited by Gary Schmidt and Susan M. Felch; Illustrations by Mary Azarian
Explore the gentle unfurling of spring and reflect on how nature celebrates rebirth and renewal. Includes Jane Kenyon, Lucy Larcom, Harry Thurston, Nathaniel Hawthorne, Noel Perrin, Annie Dillard, Martha Ballard, Barbara Kingsolver, Dorothy Wordsworth, Donald Hall, David Brill, Lionel Basney, Isak Dinesen, Paul Laurence Dunbar.
6 x 9, 352 pp, 6 b/w illus., HC, 978-1-59473-114-3 **$21.99**

Summer: A Spiritual Biography of the Season
Edited by Gary Schmidt and Susan M. Felch; Illustrations by Barry Moser
"A sumptuous banquet.... These selections lift up an exquisite wholeness found within an everyday sophistication."— ★ *Publishers Weekly* starred review
Includes Anne Lamott, Luci Shaw, Ray Bradbury, Richard Selzer, Thomas Lynch, Walt Whitman, Carl Sandburg, Sherman Alexie, Madeleine L'Engle, Jamaica Kincaid.
6 x 9, 304 pp, 5 b/w illus., HC, 978-1-59473-083-2 **$21.99**

Winter: A Spiritual Biography of the Season
Edited by Gary Schmidt and Susan M. Felch; Illustrations by Barry Moser
"This outstanding anthology features top-flight nature and spirituality writers on the fierce, inexorable season of winter.... Remarkably lively and warm, despite the icy subject." — ★ *Publishers Weekly* starred review.
Includes Will Campbell, Rachel Carson, Annie Dillard, Donald Hall, Ron Hansen, Jane Kenyon, Jamaica Kincaid, Barry Lopez, Kathleen Norris, John Updike, E. B. White.
6 x 9, 288 pp, 6 b/w illus., Deluxe PB w/flaps, 978-1-893361-92-8 **$18.95**
HC, 978-1-893361-53-9 **$21.95**

Spirituality / Animal Companions

Blessing the Animals: Prayers and Ceremonies to Celebrate God's Creatures, Wild and Tame *Edited by Lynn L. Caruso* 5 x 7¼, 256 pp, HC, 978-1-59473-145-7 **$19.99**

What Animals Can Teach Us about Spirituality: Inspiring Lessons from Wild and Tame Creatures *by Diana L. Guerrero* 6 x 9, 176 pp, Quality PB, 978-1-893361-84-3 **$16.95**

Children's Spirituality—Board Books

Adam and Eve's New Day (A Board Book)
by Sandy Eisenberg Sasso; Full-color illus. by Joani Keller Rothenberg
A lesson in hope for every child who has worried about what comes next. Abridged from *Adam and Eve's First Sunset*.
5 x 5, 24 pp, Full-color illus., Board Book, 978-1-59473-205-8 **$7.99** *For ages 0–4*

How Did the Animals Help God? (A Board Book)
by Nancy Sohn Swartz; Full-color illus. by Melanie Hall
Abridged from *In Our Image*, God asks all of nature to offer gifts to humankind—with a promise that they will care for creation in return.
5 x 5, 24 pp, Board Book, Full-color illus., 978-1-59473-044-3 **$7.99** *For ages 0–4*

Where Is God? (A Board Book) *by Lawrence and Karen Kushner; Full-color illus. by Dawn W. Majewski* A gentle way for young children to explore how God is with us every day, in every way. Abridged from *Because Nothing Looks Like God*.
5 x 5, 24 pp, Board Book, Full-color illus., 978-1-893361-17-1 **$7.99** *For ages 0–4*

What Does God Look Like? (A Board Book)
by Lawrence and Karen Kushner; Full-color illus. by Dawn W. Majewski
A simple way for young children to explore the ways that we "see" God. Abridged from *Because Nothing Looks Like God*.
5 x 5, 24 pp, Board Book, Full-color illus., 978-1-893361-23-2 **$7.95** *For ages 0–4*

How Does God Make Things Happen? (A Board Book)
by Lawrence and Karen Kushner; Full-color illus. by Dawn W. Majewski
A charming invitation for young children to explore how God makes things happen in our world. Abridged from *Because Nothing Looks Like God*.
5 x 5, 24 pp, Board Book, Full-color illus., 978-1-893361-24-9 **$7.95** *For ages 0–4*

What Is God's Name? (A Board Book)
by Sandy Eisenberg Sasso; Full-color illus. by Phoebe Stone
Everyone and everything in the world has a name. What is God's name? Abridged from the award-winning *In God's Name*.
5 x 5, 24 pp, Board Book, Full-color illus., 978-1-893361-10-2 **$7.99** *For ages 0–4*

What You Will See Inside ...

This important new series of books, each with many full-color photos, is designed to show children ages 6 and up the Who, What, When, Where, Why and How of traditional houses of worship, liturgical celebrations, and rituals of different world faiths, empowering them to respect and understand their own religious traditions—and those of their friends and neighbors.

What You Will See Inside a Catholic Church
by Reverend Michael Keane; Foreword by Robert J. Keeley, EdD
Full-color photos by Aaron Pepis
8½ x 10½, 32 pp, Full-color photos, HC, 978-1-893361-54-6 **$17.95**

Also available in Spanish: **Lo que se puede ver dentro de una iglesia católica**
8½ x 10½, 32 pp, Full-color photos, HC, 978-1-893361-66-9 **$16.95**

What You Will See Inside a Hindu Temple
by Dr. Mahendra Jani and Dr. Vandana Jani; Full-color photos by Neirah Bhargava and Vijay Dave
8½ x 10½, 32 pp, Full-color photos, HC, 978-1-59473-116-7 **$17.99**

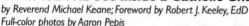

What You Will See Inside a Mosque
by Aisha Karen Khan; Full-color photos by Aaron Pepis
8½ x 10½, 32 pp, Full-color photos, HC, 978-1-893361-60-7 **$16.95**

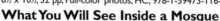

What You Will See Inside a Synagogue
by Rabbi Lawrence A. Hoffman and Dr. Ron Wolfson; Full-color photos by Bill Aron
8½ x 10½, 32 pp, Full-color photos, HC, 978-1-59473-012-2 **$17.99**

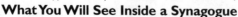

Children's Spirituality

Remembering My Grandparent: A Kid's Own Grief Workbook in the Christian Tradition *by Nechama Liss-Levinson, PhD, and Rev. Molly Phinney Baskette, MDiv*
8 x 10, 48 pp, 2-color text, HC, 978-1-59473-212-6 **$16.99** *For ages 7–13*

Does God Ever Sleep? *by Joan Sauro, CSJ; Full-color photos*
A charming nighttime reminder that God is always present in our lives.
10 x 8½, 32 pp, Quality PB, Full-color photos, 978-1-59473-110-5 **$8.99** *For ages 3–6*

Does God Forgive Me? *by August Gold; Full-color photos by Diane Hardy Waller*
Gently shows how God forgives all that we do if we are truly sorry.
10 x 8½, 32 pp, Quality PB, Full-color photos, 978-1-59473-142-6 **$8.99** *For ages 3–6*

God Said Amen *by Sandy Eisenberg Sasso; Full-color illus. by Avi Katz*
A warm and inspiring tale of two kingdoms that shows us that we need only reach out to each other to find the answers to our prayers.
9 x 12, 32 pp, HC, Full-color illus., 978-1-58023-080-3 **$16.95**
For ages 4 & up (a Jewish Lights book)

How Does God Listen? *by Kay Lindahl; Full-color photos by Cynthia Maloney*
How do we know when God is listening to us? Children will find the answers to these questions as they engage their senses while the story unfolds, learning how God listens in the wind, waves, clouds, hot chocolate, perfume, our tears and our laughter.
10 x 8½, 32 pp, Quality PB, Full-color photos, 978-1-59473-084-9 **$8.99** *For ages 3–6*

In God's Hands *by Lawrence Kushner and Gary Schmidt; Full-color illus. by Matthew J. Baeck*
9 x 12, 32 pp, Full-color illus., HC, 978-1-58023-224-1 **$16.99** *For ages 5 & up (a Jewish Lights book)*

In God's Name *by Sandy Eisenberg Sasso; Full-color illus. by Phoebe Stone*
Like an ancient myth in its poetic text and vibrant illustrations, this award-winning modern fable about the search for God's name celebrates the diversity and, at the same time, the unity of all the people of the world.
9 x 12, 32 pp, HC, Full-color illus., 978-1-879045-26-2 **$16.99**
For ages 4 & up (a Jewish Lights book)

Also available in Spanish: **El nombre de Dios**
9 x 12, 32 pp, HC, Full-color illus., 978-1-893361-63-8 **$16.95**

In Our Image: God's First Creatures
by Nancy Sohn Swartz; Full-color illus. by Melanie Hall
A playful new twist on the Genesis story—from the perspective of the animals. Celebrates the interconnectedness of nature and the harmony of all living things. 9 x 12, 32 pp, HC, Full-color illus., 978-1-879045-99-6 **$16.95**
For ages 4 & up (a Jewish Lights book)

Noah's Wife: The Story of Naamah
by Sandy Eisenberg Sasso; Full-color illus. by Bethanne Andersen
This new story, based on an ancient text, opens readers' religious imaginations to new ideas about the well-known story of the Flood. When God tells Noah to bring the animals of the world onto the ark, God also calls on Naamah, Noah's wife, to save each plant on Earth.
9 x 12, 32 pp, HC, Full-color illus., 978-1-58023-134-3 **$16.95**
For ages 4 & up (a Jewish Lights book)

Also available: **Naamah:** Noah's Wife (A Board Book)
by Sandy Eisenberg Sasso; Full-color illus. by Bethanne Andersen
5 x 5, 24 pp, Board Book, Full-color illus., 978-1-893361-56-0 **$7.99** *For ages 0–4*

Where Does God Live? *by August Gold and Matthew J. Perlman*
Using simple, everyday examples that children can relate to, this colorful book helps young readers develop a personal understanding of God.
10 x 8½, 32 pp, Quality PB, Full-color photo illus., 978-1-893361-39-3 **$8.99** *For ages 3–6*

Sacred Texts—SkyLight Illuminations Series
Andrew Harvey, Series Editor

Offers today's spiritual seeker an accessible entry into the great classic texts of the world's spiritual traditions. Each classic is presented in an accessible translation, with facing pages of guided commentary from experts, giving you the keys you need to understand the history, context and meaning of the text. This series enables you, whatever your background, to experience and understand classic spiritual texts directly, and to make them a part of your life.

CHRISTIANITY

The End of Days: Essential Selections from Apocalyptic Texts— Annotated & Explained   *Annotation by Robert G. Clouse*
Introduces you to the beliefs and values held by those who rely on the promises found in the Book of Revelation. 5½ x 8½, 192 pp, Quality PB, 978-1-59473-170-9 **$16.99**

The Hidden Gospel of Matthew: Annotated & Explained
Translation & Annotation by Ron Miller
Takes you deep into the text cherished around the world to discover the words and events that have the strongest connection to the historical Jesus.
5½ x 8½, 272 pp, Quality PB, 978-1-59473-038-2 **$16.99**

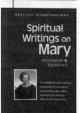

The Lost Sayings of Jesus: Teachings from Ancient Christian, Jewish, Gnostic and Islamic Sources—Annotated & Explained
Translation & Annotation by Andrew Phillip Smith; Foreword by Stephan A. Hoeller
This collection of more than three hundred sayings depicts Jesus as a Wisdom teacher who speaks to people of all faiths as a mystic and spiritual master.
5½ x 8½, 240 pp, Quality PB, 978-1-59473-172-3 **$16.99**

Philokalia: The Eastern Christian Spiritual Texts—Selections Annotated & Explained   *Annotation by Allyne Smith; Foreword by Bishop Kallistos Ware*
The first approachable introduction to the wisdom of the Philokalia, which is the classic text of Eastern Christian spirituality.
5½ x 8½, 176 pp, Quality PB, 978-1-59473-103-7 **$16.99**

Spiritual Writings on Mary: Annotated & Explained
Annotation by Mary Ford-Grabowsky; Foreword by Andrew Harvey
Examines the role of Mary, the mother of Jesus, as a source of inspiration in history and in life today. 5½ x 8½, 288 pp, Quality PB, 978-1-59473-001-6 **$16.99**

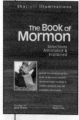

The Way of a Pilgrim: Annotated & Explained
Translation & Annotation by Gleb Pokrovsky; Foreword by Andrew Harvey
This classic of Russian spirituality is the delightful account of one man who sets out to learn the prayer of the heart, also known as the "Jesus prayer."
5½ x 8½, 160 pp, Illus., Quality PB, 978-1-893361-31-7 **$14.95**

MORMONISM

The Book of Mormon: Selections Annotated & Explained
Annotation by Jana Riess; Foreword by Phyllis Tickle
Explores the sacred epic that is cherished by more than twelve million members of the LDS church as the keystone of their faith.
5½ x 8½ , 272 pp, Quality PB, 978-1-59473-076-4 **$16.99**

NATIVE AMERICAN

Native American Stories of the Sacred: Annotated & Explained
Retold & Annotated by Evan T. Pritchard
Intended for more than entertainment, these teaching tales contain elegantly simple illustrations of time-honored truths.
5½ x 8½, 272 pp, Quality PB, 978-1-59473-112-9 **$16.99**

Sacred Texts—cont.

GNOSTICISM

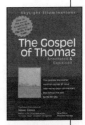

The Gospel of Philip: Annotated & Explained
Translation & Annotation by Andrew Phillip Smith; Foreword by Stevan Davies
Reveals otherwise unrecorded sayings of Jesus and fragments of Gnostic mythology.
5½ x 8½, 160 pp, Quality PB, 978-1-59473-111-2 **$16.99**

The Gospel of Thomas: Annotated & Explained
Translation & Annotation by Stevan Davies Sheds new light on the origins of Christianity and portrays Jesus as a wisdom-loving sage. 5½ x 8½, 192 pp, Quality PB, 978-1-893361-45-4 **$16.99**

The Secret Book of John: The Gnostic Gospel—Annotated & Explained
Translation & Annotation by Stevan Davies The most significant and influential text of the ancient Gnostic religion. 5½ x 8½, 208 pp, Quality PB, 978-1-59473-082-5 **$16.99**

JUDAISM

The Divine Feminine in Biblical Wisdom Literature
Selections Annotated & Explained
Translation & Annotation by Rabbi Rami Shapiro; Foreword by Rev. Cynthia Bourgeault, PhD
Uses the Hebrew books of Psalms, Proverbs, Song of Songs, Ecclesiastes and Job, Wisdom literature and the Wisdom of Solomon to clarify who Wisdom is.
5½ x 8½, 240 pp, Quality PB, 978-1-59473-109-9 **$16.99**

Ethics of the Sages: Pirke Avot—Annotated & Explained
Translation & Annotation by Rabbi Rami Shapiro Clarifies the ethical teachings of the early Rabbis. 5½ x 8½, 192 pp, Quality PB, 978-1-59473-207-2 **$16.99**

Hasidic Tales: Annotated & Explained
Translation & Annotation by Rabbi Rami Shapiro
Introduces the legendary tales of the impassioned Hasidic rabbis, presenting them as stories rather than as parables. 5½ x 8½, 240 pp, Quality PB, 978-1-893361-86-7 **$16.95**

The Hebrew Prophets: Selections Annotated & Explained
Translation & Annotation by Rabbi Rami Shapiro; Foreword by Zalman M. Schachter-Shalomi
Focuses on the central themes covered by all the Hebrew prophets.
5½ x 8½, 224 pp, Quality PB, 978-1-59473-037-5 **$16.99**

Zohar: Annotated & Explained *Translation & Annotation by Daniel C. Matt*
The best-selling author of *The Essential Kabbalah* brings together in one place the most important teachings of the Zohar, the canonical text of Jewish mystical tradition.
5½ x 8½, 176 pp, Quality PB, 978-1-893361-51-5 **$15.99**

EASTERN RELIGIONS

Bhagavad Gita: Annotated & Explained *Translation by Shri Purohit Swami*
Annotation by Kendra Crossen Burroughs Explains references and philosophical terms, shares the interpretations of famous spiritual leaders and scholars, and more.
5½ x 8½, 192 pp, Quality PB, 978-1-893361-28-7 **$16.95**

Dhammapada: Annotated & Explained *Translation by Max Müller and revised by*
Jack Maguire; Annotation by Jack Maguire Contains all of Buddhism's key teachings.
5½ x 8½, 160 pp, b/w photos, Quality PB, 978-1-893361-42-3 **$14.95**

Rumi and Islam: Selections from His Stories, Poems, and Discourses—
Annotated & Explained *Translation & Annotation by Ibrahim Gamard*
Focuses on Rumi's place within the Sufi tradition of Islam, providing insight into the mystical side of the religion. 5½ x 8½, 240 pp, Quality PB, 978-1-59473-002-3 **$15.99**

Selections from the Gospel of Sri Ramakrishna: Annotated & Explained
Translation by Swami Nikhilananda; Annotation by Kendra Crossen Burroughs
Introduces the fascinating world of the Indian mystic and the universal appeal of his message. 5½ x 8½, 240 pp, b/w photos, Quality PB, 978-1-893361-46-1 **$16.95**

Tao Te Ching: Annotated & Explained *Translation & Annotation by Derek Lin*
Introduces an Eastern classic in an accessible, poetic and completely original way.
5½ x 8½, 192 pp, Quality PB, 978-1-59473-204-1 **$16.99**

Spirituality

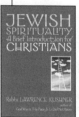

Jewish Spirituality: A Brief Introduction for Christians *by Lawrence Kushner*
5½ x 8½, 112 pp, Quality PB, 978-1-58023-150-3 **$12.95** *(a Jewish Lights book)*

Journeys of Simplicity: Traveling Light with Thomas Merton, Bashō, Edward Abbey, Annie Dillard & Others *by Philip Harnden* 5 x 7¼, 128 pp, HC, 978-1-893361-76-8 **$16.95**

Keeping Spiritual Balance As We Grow Older: More than 65 Creative Ways to Use Purpose, Prayer, and the Power of Spirit to Build a Meaningful Retirement *by Molly and Bernie Srode* 8 x 8, 224 pp, Quality PB, 978-1-59473-042-9 **$16.99**

The Monks of Mount Athos: A Western Monk's Extraordinary Spiritual Journey on Eastern Holy Ground *by M. Basil Pennington, ocso; Foreword by Archimandrite Dionysios*
6 x 9, 256 pp, 10+ b/w line drawings, Quality PB, 978-1-893361-78-2 **$18.95**

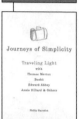

One God Clapping: The Spiritual Path of a Zen Rabbi *by Alan Lew with Sherrill Jaffe*
5½ x 8½, 336 pp, Quality PB, 978-1-58023-115-2 **$16.95** *(a Jewish Lights book)*

Prayer for People Who Think Too Much: A Guide to Everyday, Anywhere Prayer from the World's Faith Traditions *by Mitch Finley*
5½ x 8½, 224 pp, Quality PB, 978-1-893361-21-8 **$16.99**; HC, 978-1-893361-00-3 **$21.95**

Show Me Your Way: The Complete Guide to Exploring Interfaith Spiritual Direction *by Howard A. Addison* 5½ x 8½, 240 pp, Quality PB, 978-1-893361-41-6 **$16.95**

Spirituality 101: The Indispensable Guide to Keeping—or Finding—Your Spiritual Life on Campus *by Harriet L. Schwartz, with contributions from college students at nearly thirty campuses across the United States* 6 x 9, 272 pp, Quality PB, 978-1-59473-000-9 **$16.99**

Spiritually Incorrect: Finding God in All the Wrong Places *by Dan Wakefield; Illus. by Marian DelVecchio* 5½ x 8½, 192 pp, b/w illus., Quality PB, 978-1-59473-137-2 **$15.99**

Spiritual Manifestos: Visions for Renewed Religious Life in America from Young Spiritual Leaders of Many Faiths *Edited by Niles Elliot Goldstein; Preface by Martin E. Marty*
6 x 9, 256 pp, HC, 978-1-893361-09-6 **$21.95**

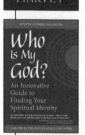

A Walk with Four Spiritual Guides: Krishna, Buddha, Jesus, and Ramakrishna *by Andrew Harvey* 5½ x 8½, 192 pp, 10 b/w photos & illus., Quality PB, 978-1-59473-138-9 **$15.99**

What Matters: Spiritual Nourishment for Head and Heart *by Frederick Franck* 5 x 7¼, 128 pp, 50+ b/w illus., HC, 978-1-59473-013-9 **$16.99**

Who Is My God?, 2nd Edition: An Innovative Guide to Finding Your Spiritual Identity *Created by the Editors at SkyLight Paths* 6 x 9, 160 pp, Quality PB, 978-1-59473-014-6 **$15.99**

Spirituality—A Week Inside

Come and Sit: A Week Inside Meditation Centers
by Marcia Z. Nelson; Foreword by Wayne Teasdale
The insider's guide to meditation in a variety of different spiritual traditions—Buddhist, Hindu, Christian, Jewish, and Sufi traditions.
6 x 9, 224 pp, b/w photos, Quality PB, 978-1-893361-35-5 **$16.95**

Lighting the Lamp of Wisdom: A Week Inside a Yoga Ashram
by John Ittner; Foreword by Dr. David Frawley
This insider's guide to Hindu spiritual life takes you into a typical week of retreat inside a yoga ashram to demystify the experience and show you what to expect.
6 x 9, 192 pp, 10+ b/w photos, Quality PB, 978-1-893361-52-2 **$15.95**

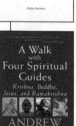

Making a Heart for God: A Week Inside a Catholic Monastery
by Dianne Aprile; Foreword by Brother Patrick Hart, ocso
Takes you to the Abbey of Gethsemani—the Trappist monastery in Kentucky that was home to author Thomas Merton—to explore the details.
6 x 9, 224 pp, b/w photos, Quality PB, 978-1-893361-49-2 **$16.95**

Waking Up: A Week Inside a Zen Monastery
by Jack Maguire; Foreword by John Daido Loori, Roshi
An essential guide to what it's like to spend a week inside a Zen Buddhist monastery.
6 x 9, 224 pp, b/w photos, Quality PB, 978-1-893361-55-3 **$16.95**
HC, 978-1-893361-13-3 **$21.95**

Midrash Fiction / Folktales

Abraham's Bind & Other Bible Tales of Trickery, Folly, Mercy and Love *by Michael J. Caduto*
New retellings of episodes in the lives of familiar biblical characters explore relevant life lessons.
6 x 9, 192 pp, HC, 978-1-59473-186-0 **$19.99**

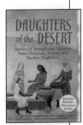

Daughters of the Desert: Stories of Remarkable Women from Christian, Jewish and Muslim Traditions *by Claire Rudolf Murphy, Meghan Nuttall Sayres, Mary Cronk Farrell, Sarah Conover and Betsy Wharton*
Breathes new life into the old tales of our female ancestors in faith. Uses traditional scriptural passages as starting points, then with vivid detail fills in historical context and place. Chapters reveal the voices of Sarah, Hagar, Huldah, Esther, Salome, Mary Magdalene, Lydia, Khadija, Fatima and many more. Historical fiction ideal for readers of all ages. Quality paperback includes reader's discussion guide.
5½ x 8½, 192 pp, Quality PB, 978-1-59473-106-8 **$14.99**
HC, 192 pp, 978-1-893361-72-0 **$19.95**

The Triumph of Eve & Other Subversive Bible Tales
by Matt Biers-Ariel
Many people were taught and remember only a one-dimensional Bible. These engaging retellings are the antidote to this—they're witty, often hilarious, always profound, and invite you to grapple with questions and issues that are often hidden in the original text.
5½ x 8½, 192 pp, HC, 978-1-59473-040-5 **$19.99**

Also avail.: **The Triumph of Eve Teacher's Guide**
8½ x 11, 44 pp, PB, 978-1-59473-152-5 **$8.99**

Wisdom in the Telling
Finding Inspiration and Grace in Traditional Folktales and Myths Retold
by Lorraine Hartin-Gelardi
6 x 9, 224 pp, HC, 978-1-59473-185-3 **$19.99**

Religious Etiquette / Reference

How to Be a Perfect Stranger, 4th Edition: The Essential Religious Etiquette Handbook *Edited by Stuart M. Matlins and Arthur J. Magida*
The indispensable guidebook to help the well-meaning guest when visiting other people's religious ceremonies. A straightforward guide to the rituals and celebrations of the major religions and denominations in the United States and Canada from the perspective of an interested guest of any other faith, based on information obtained from authorities of each religion. Belongs in every living room, library and office. Covers:
African American Methodist Churches • Assemblies of God • Bahá'í • Baptist • Buddhist • Christian Church (Disciples of Christ) • Christian Science (Church of Christ, Scientist) • Churches of Christ • Episcopalian and Anglican • Hindu • Islam • Jehovah's Witnesses • Jewish • Lutheran • Mennonite/Amish • Methodist • Mormon (Church of Jesus Christ of Latter-day Saints) • Native American/First Nations • Orthodox Churches • Pentecostal Church of God • Presbyterian • Quaker (Religious Society of Friends) • Reformed Church in America/Canada • Roman Catholic • Seventh-day Adventist • Sikh • Unitarian Universalist • United Church of Canada • United Church of Christ
6 x 9, 432 pp, Quality PB, 978-1-59473-140-2 **$19.99**

The Perfect Stranger's Guide to Funerals and Grieving Practices: A Guide to Etiquette in Other People's Religious Ceremonies *Edited by Stuart M. Matlins*
6 x 9, 240 pp, Quality PB, 978-1-893361-20-1 **$16.95**

The Perfect Stranger's Guide to Wedding Ceremonies: A Guide to Etiquette in Other People's Religious Ceremonies *Edited by Stuart M. Matlins*
6 x 9, 208 pp, Quality PB, 978-1-893361-19-5 **$16.95**

Spirituality & Craft

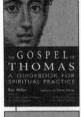

The Knitting Way: A Guide to Spiritual Self-Discovery
by Linda Skolnik and Janice MacDaniels
7 x 9, 240 pp, Quality PB, 978-1-59473-079-5 **$16.99**

The Quilting Path
A Guide to Spiritual Discovery through Fabric, Thread and Kabbalah
by Louise Silk
7 x 9, 192 pp, Quality PB, 978-1-59473-206-5 **$16.99**

Spiritual Practice

Divining the Body
Reclaim the Holiness of Your Physical Self *by Jan Phillips*
A practical and inspiring guidebook for connecting the body and soul in spiritual practice. Leads you into a milieu of reverence, mystery and delight, helping you discover your body as a pathway to the Divine.
8 x 8, 256 pp, Quality PB, 978-1-59473-080-1 **$16.99**

Finding Time for the Timeless: Spirituality in the Workweek
by John McQuiston II
Simple, refreshing stories that provide you with examples of how you can refocus and enrich your daily life using prayer or meditation, ritual and other forms of spiritual practice. 5½ x 6¼, 208 pp, HC, 978-1-59473-035-1 **$17.99**

The Gospel of Thomas
A Guidebook for Spiritual Practice *by Ron Miller; Translations by Stevan Davies*
An innovative guide to bring a new spiritual classic into daily life.
6 x 9, 160 pp, Quality PB, 978-1-59473-047-4 **$14.99**

Earth, Water, Fire, and Air: Essential Ways of Connecting to Spirit
by Cait Johnson 6 x 9, 224 pp, HC, 978-1-893361-65-2 **$19.95**

Everyday Herbs in Spiritual Life: A Guide to Many Practices
by Ana Hernández and Susan F. Jones 5½ x 8½, 176 pp, Quality PB, 978-1-59473-174-7 **$16.99**

Labyrinths from the Outside In: Walking to Spiritual Insight—A Beginner's Guide
by Donna Schaper and Carole Ann Camp
6 x 9, 208 pp, b/w illus. and photos, Quality PB, 978-1-893361-18-8 **$16.95**

Practicing the Sacred Art of Listening: A Guide to Enrich Your Relationships
and Kindle Your Spiritual Life—The Listening Center Workshop
by Kay Lindahl 8 x 8, 176 pp, Quality PB, 978-1-893361-85-0 **$16.95**

Releasing the Creative Spirit: Unleash the Creativity in Your Life
by Dan Wakefield 7 x 10, 256 pp, Quality PB, 978-1-893361-36-2 **$16.95**

The Sacred Art of Bowing: Preparing to Practice
by Andi Young 5½ x 8½, 128 pp, b/w illus., Quality PB, 978-1-893361-82-9 **$14.95**

The Sacred Art of Chant: Preparing to Practice
by Ana Hernández 5½ x 8½, 192 pp, Quality PB, 978-1-59473-036-8 **$15.99**

The Sacred Art of Fasting: Preparing to Practice
by Thomas Ryan, CSP 5½ x 8½, 192 pp, Quality PB, 978-1-59473-078-8 **$15.99**

The Sacred Art of Forgiveness: Forgiving Ourselves and Others through God's Grace
by Marcia Ford 8 x 8, 176 pp, Quality PB, 978-1-59473-175-4 **$16.99**

The Sacred Art of Listening: Forty Reflections for Cultivating a Spiritual Practice
by Kay Lindahl; Illustrations by Amy Schnapper
8 x 8, 160 pp, b/w illus., Quality PB, 978-1-893361-44-7 **$16.99**

The Sacred Art of Lovingkindness: Preparing to Practice
by Rabbi Rami Shapiro; Foreword by Marcia Ford
5½ x 8½, 176 pp, Quality PB, 978-1-59473-151-8 **$16.99**

Sacred Speech: A Practical Guide for Keeping Spirit in Your Speech
by Rev. Donna Schaper 6 x 9, 176 pp, Quality PB, 978-1-59473-068-9 **$15.99**
HC, 978-1-893361-74-4 **$21.95**

Kabbalah from Jewish Lights Publishing

Awakening to Kabbalah: The Guiding Light of Spiritual Fulfillment
by Rav Michael Laitman, PhD 6 x 9, 192 pp, HC, 978-1-58023-264-7 **$21.99**

Cast in God's Image: Discover Your Personality Type Using the Enneagram and Kabbalah
by Rabbi Howard A. Addison 7 x 9, 176 pp, Quality PB, 978-1-58023-124-4 **$16.95**

Ehyeh: A Kabbalah for Tomorrow *by Dr. Arthur Green*
6 x 9, 224 pp, Quality PB, 978-1-58023-213-5 **$16.99**

The Enneagram and Kabbalah, 2nd Edition: Reading Your Soul
by Rabbi Howard A. Addison 6 x 9, 192 pp, Quality PB, 978-1-58023-229-6 **$16.99**

Finding Joy: A Practical Spiritual Guide to Happiness *by Dannel I. Schwartz with Mark Hass*
6 x 9, 192 pp, Quality PB, 978-1-58023-009-4 **$14.95**

The Gift of Kabbalah: Discovering the Secrets of Heaven, Renewing Your Life on Earth
by Tamar Frankiel, PhD 6 x 9, 256 pp, Quality PB, 978-1-58023-141-1 **$16.95**
HC, 978-1-58023-108-4 **$21.95**

Honey from the Rock: An Easy Introduction to Jewish Mysticism
by Lawrence Kushner 6 x 9, 176 pp, Quality PB, 978-1-58023-073-5 **$16.95**

Kabbalah: A Brief Introduction for Christians
by Tamar Frankiel, PhD 5½ x 8½, 176 pp, Quality PB, 978-1-58023-303-3 **$16.99**

Zohar: Annotated & Explained *Translation and Annotation by Dr. Daniel C. Matt*
Foreword by Andrew Harvey 5½ x 8½, 176 pp, Quality PB, 978-1-893361-51-5 **$15.99**

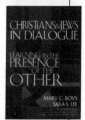

Judaism / Christianity

Christians and Jews in Dialogue: Learning in the Presence of the Other
by Mary C. Boys and Sara S. Lee; Foreword by Dorothy C. Bass
Inspires renewed commitment to dialogue between religious traditions and illuminates how it should happen. Explains the transformative work of creating environments for Jews and Christians to study together and enter the dynamism of the other's religious tradition.
6 x 9, 256 pp, HC, 978-1-59473-144-0 **$21.99**

Healing the Jewish-Christian Rift: Growing Beyond Our Wounded History
by Ron Miller and Laura Bernstein; Foreword by Dr. Beatrice Bruteau
6 x 9, 288 pp, Quality PB, 978-1-59473-139-6 **$18.99**

Introducing My Faith and My Community
The Jewish Outreach Institute Guide for the Christian in a Jewish Interfaith Relationship
by Rabbi Kerry M. Olitzky 6 x 9, 176 pp, Quality PB, 978-1-58023-192-3 **$16.99** *(a Jewish Lights book)*

The Jewish Approach to God: A Brief Introduction for Christians
by Rabbi Neil Gillman 5½ x 8½, 192 pp, Quality PB, 978-1-58023-190-9 **$16.95** *(a Jewish Lights book)*

Jewish Holidays: A Brief Introduction for Christians
by Rabbi Kerry M. Olitzky and Rabbi Daniel Judson
5½ x 8½, 176 pp, Quality PB, 978-1-58023-302-6 **$16.99** *(a Jewish Lights book)*

Jewish Ritual: A Brief Introduction for Christians
by Rabbi Kerry M. Olitzky and Rabbi Daniel Judson
5½ x 8½, 144 pp, Quality PB, 978-1-58023-210-4 **$14.99** *(a Jewish Lights book)*

Jewish Spirituality: A Brief Introduction for Christians
by Rabbi Lawrence Kushner
5½ x 8½, 112 pp, Quality PB, 978-1-58023-150-3 **$12.95** *(a Jewish Lights book)*

A Jewish Understanding of the New Testament
by Rabbi Samuel Sandmel; new Preface by Rabbi David Sandmel
5½ x 8½, 368 pp, Quality PB, 978-1-59473-048-1 **$19.99**

We Jews and Jesus
Exploring Theological Differences for Mutual Understanding
by Rabbi Samuel Sandmel; new Preface by Rabbi David Sandmel A Classic Reprint
Written in a non-technical way for the layperson, this candid and forthright look at the what and why of the Jewish attitude toward Jesus is a clear and forceful exposition that guides both Christians and Jews in relevant discussion.
6 x 9, 192 pp, Quality PB, 978-1-59473-208-9 **$16.99**